Falling into Peaces

Falling into Peaces

✦

A Memoir

Carol A. Coussons de Reyes, CPS, MS

iUniverse, Inc.

New York Bloomington Shanghai

Falling into Peaces
A Memoir

iUniverse books may be ordered through booksellers or by contacting:

iUniverse
1663 Liberty Drive
Bloomington, IN 47403
www.iuniverse.com
1-800-Authors (1-800-288-4677)

Because of the dynamic nature of the Internet, any Web addresses or links contained in this book may have changed since publication and may no longer be valid.

This book is a memoir or a longer version of a recovery story. It is meant to be read as one person's journey and not professional instruction or advice. I have written this as a peer with the understanding that each and everyone of my peers is free to make their own decisions in life. Neither the author nor the publisher shall be liable or responsible for any loss or damage allegedly arising as a consequence of your use or application of any information in this book.

ISBN: 978-0-595-46596-5 (pbk)
ISBN: 978-0-595-70366-1 (cloth)
ISBN: 978-0-595-90892-9 (ebk)

Printed in the United States of America

To Gabriel, my angel:

Like a new blossom on an orchid thought dead,
Love steps in the room and rears its glorious head.
Bursting wide open from a closed state,
The crying inside exits in grace.
Green and fuchsia bleed into each other,
Like the pigments of our hands together.
Singing from a very high place on the stalk,
From above perpetually we shall walk.
For when this fragile flower meets its doom,
Our love will be springing into bloom.

To My Grandmother:
Thank you for communicating the support of your congregation during my dark hours.

To My Peers:
Writing a book is like looking at my reflection in a mirror; it never seems quite right. There is always something to change. I have paid to publish this book and I must release it. I hope that it brings people who I know and have yet to know closer together.

To Spiritual Leaders of Faith and Respect for Others' Faiths:
Do not be so comfortable passing the work of serious matters that relate to mental health off to a doctor alone. It is a psychologist who told me not to go to church. It is a hospital that denied me a place of adoration at the time I needed it most. Often it is a regular mission to visit those in prison and hospitals for the physically ill; come and knock on the doors of the remaining institutions of mental health.

To Dr. Alta Eblin:
Thank you for being there with me and not above me.

To Marie Gonzalez:
Thank you for believing.

To Mom and Dad:
I love you both.

Contents

Preface

Mental health affects many of our lives. For some people, it impinges on the lives of their brothers, sisters, uncles, aunts, or cousins. For others, as taxpayers they pay for mental health services. Whatever one's experience, citizens of the United States and the world need to know what is going on in the mental health field.

For many years, researchers and doctors taught us most of what we knew about mental health. We did not hear from the individuals receiving services. The people consuming mental health services often were passively obedient to their doctors. Further, many people were warehoused in hospitals, locked away from the world. Many individuals died silently and faceless to their communities at the very institutions that were to restore their health. There was a sharp divide between us, the sane, and them, the mentally ill.

Much has changed in the world. The long history of warehousing the mentally ill has come face to face with the demand for individual civil rights. People are reclaiming these rights that date back to the Declaration of Independence and our founding fathers.

This reclaiming of rights is called the "consumer movement." Consumers of mental health services are speaking out and being heard. They can be found today telling their doctors how they feel and what medication they want to take. They are in courts of law, telling judges where they want to live. They are on treatment teams, telling providers how they want to receive services. Consumers of mental health services are providers themselves. They are partnering with their community to create new and innovative roads to wellness. Today, there is a national movement by consumers to reclaim the sacred and mark forgotten burial grounds of those who walked before them.

Further, in our country there is a movement toward recovery. The executive summary vision statement in the president's New Freedom Commission Report on Mental Health reads: "We envision a future when everyone with mental illness will recover, a future when mental illness can be prevented or cured ..." The word *recovery* can be found on the lips of mental health associations across the United States. Recovery means that one can lead a meaningful life in the community. It implies that one's health improves but not in a linear fashion. One may experience a low-point that some would refer to as a relapse and still be on the road of recovery: it is a journey. The notion of this pursuit of recovery was borrowed from those who live with addictive disease and come together in support groups.

The pursuit of recovery for individuals with mental health issues is primarily supported by peers with similar issues. There are support groups all over the country working to nurture people's recovery.

There are also individuals with mental health issues who are referred to as peer specialists within the mental health system. Some are certified and others are uncertified. Medicaid currently pays for certified peer specialists, and those specialists are considered valuable members in the transformation of the American mental health system to the recovery model. They are being paid because their individual journeys impart knowledge that cannot be learned from textbooks. The individual experience is completely different from a list of symptoms in a book, just as anyone's life cannot be defined by whatever illness he or she is labeled with.

We do not consider the description of diabetes or cancer to define everything about a person, yet often mental health issues are seen as defining the individual's character. They receive labels that become their lives. An individual living with schizophrenia, for example, may be viewed by himself and others as a person who has an illness, takes medications, and goes to psychosocial rehabilitation. People forget everything else about the individual's life and refer to him or her as a "schizophrenic". This is the act of stigmatization that can be inflicted by others or even by the individual themselves.

This stigma is furthered because, in our culture, people view our lives through the treatment model instead of a recovery model. In the treatment model, people see us as diseased individuals that must take medication for the rest of our lives. This model does not acknowledge that some people experience recovery without medication. The treatment model does not acknowledge or celebrate the wellness of people that take medications and experience recovery. It also overlooks the role that the environment and people can play in people's lives. Supportive environments that foster recovery can result in an individual living a life where they are only experiencing the ordinary stress that everyone else does. Acknowledging the possibilities that exist in one's self and the environment is what the recovery model does, in essence.

By creating hope in people's lives and affirming that it is possible to recover, many are attaining lives in the community instead of being warehoused in hospitals. Service systems are moving into the community. Consumers of mental health services are becoming visible and speaking. Those with lived experience with mental health issues are at conferences where individuals gather to speak about what is working and what is challenging.

My life has been changed by the recovery model and the consumer movement, and I tell my story in this book. Readers will learn what it is like to live with a mental health issue. Others took my civil rights away from me in fear, as I was hospitalized for almost a month in the state of Connecticut. When I came home to Georgia, medical professionals at the state hospital quickly recognized that I belonged in the community and returned me there. Further, in Georgia I was trained by the state's Consumer Relations and Recovery Section in the recovery model. The Georgia Mental Health Consumer Network, a robust recovery-oriented consumer advocacy group, partnered in this training.

My environment did not fully change until I received this training because family and doctors were grounded in the treatment model. I'm not implying that treatment does not have a place, but this book will demonstrate the power of recovery.

I say that the team that hospitalized me in Connecticut took away my civil rights in fear because I feel fear was one of the underlying factors that kept me hospitalized. When we act in love of our fellow man, there is so much more we can do than hospitalizing people who are acting differently. In love, we can see that it is okay for someone to make their own choices once they are released from our care. In love, we see people as fully human and not as walking diseases. In love, we listen to what the individual wants, not what we want. In fear, we hold onto others with a rigid grip and hospitalize or jail people for small reasons. We see every negative thing that could happen to them in the world and overlook potential positive outcomes.

Those who react out of fear are like overprotective parents, like those I was raised by. Restrictive environments do not allow individuals to develop their own identities. They can suffocate the very voice of the individual because everyone acts out of fear that the individual may make a wrong choice. This can result in the restricted individual feeling anger instead of compassion for others.

When we love people, we allow them to experience their own choices and challenges. We are there when they falter and listen with compassion. We listen for what the individual has learned from their challenge. We search inside ourselves and see what we have in our own experience that we could share. For people that we love, we take time away from the things that busy us for these exchanges. One day the individual is so strong, full of compassion, and full of experience with challenges that they are free to choose a life of their own.

Those that live with mental health issues are often missing love and acceptance in their environment. Their families and the community at large act out of fear of and for the individual instead of love. Communities are haunted by the media, which presents the most frightening scenarios and often does not share front-page and prime-time space with uplifting stories.

But peers in support groups and in peer support services are giving each other positive affirmation of each other's struggles and existence in life. When treatment teams, the community, advocates, and families act by affirming what individuals have learned through their own struggles and journeys, we will have truly have created a revolution. That revolution will be not acting in fear and suffocating the life from people but in love that celebrates the life and the struggle of each unique and valued individual.

In this work, I take the reader to the beginning of everything. It may not be the true essence of "everything," because I had some horrible childhood experiences that I do not describe. What I do describe is the essence of a storm that was created in my life by what doctor's refer to as bipolar disorder. This storm was out of my control, as you will see.

This book will tell the reader about the great torment of this storm and the positive events that arose from it. I consider this experience the greatest gift that God could have given me and not a disease of unlucky genetics.

Introduction:
The Gift

Prepare yourself for a journey into my mind. You will experience blow by blow what it is like to live with a mental health issue. For years I have struggled with what doctors call mental illness. Part of this book was written at times when I could barely utter a sentence because I was so depressed. Yet I had great energy to share this dark experience. There are rocky moments written when my mind was jumping from place to place. In these moments I describe mammoth fears, sadness, pain, and beauty. Doctors have used medical language to call this a mixed state of bipolar disorder, meaning I experienced sadness and had great energy all at once.

There is a great art to being me; I have lived through so much. Before my mental health issues began, I used to think that bipolar disorder afflicted people who had experienced so much that their bodies or minds just couldn't handle it. I still wonder if that is true. Some days I am amazed that I am alive. In Georgia's Certified Peer Specialist training, my peers and I were called "a walking miracle." I often wear a button that says this to remind myself. It has taken so much hard work to get to where I am now.

My life has been an adventure that I never seemed to choose on my own. I was lost in a tangle of strange situations and characters, some of which I will never speak of. I can say my past is great. I reveal what I can, and, for some people, that is a lot.

I've had so much psychotherapy that I refuse to go to any more psychotherapists. I figure after fourteen years of such therapy and attaining a master's degree in psychology, there is nothing left that they can teach me. Occasionally, social workers seem to understand me better. A psychiatrist has been a must in my life. My relationship with my current doctor is not a passive one; he sits on the couch, and I sit in the chair. I started our sessions with a copy of the president's New Freedom Commission Report and stated that I wanted to work on recovery without medication. There are people like that out there.

I don't know where I would be without my family. They have never given up. While far from perfect, they have broken into my house to pay the bills while I was miles away from home. My mother and father have taken money out of their retirement savings to get me over the humps. If it weren't for them, I wouldn't have many of the material things that I do today. While I do not appreciate everything that my parents have done, I am glad that the National Alliance on Mental Illness and the Depression and Bipolar Support Alliance were there to support them.

There are many great people in Georgia that have supported my return from the great unknown, particularly the Georgia Mental Health Consumer Network and the Consumer Relations and Recovery Section of the Department of Human Resources: Division of Mental Health, Developmental Disabilities, and Addictive Diseases. Through their certified peer specialist training, I have found things inside myself that I could not voice on my own; things that my parents and doctors didn't know to tell me.

A great truth has revealed itself to me in the last few years of my life: I am gifted, not ill. At times, my ego is off the charts and my doctors have named this mania. I have named this my great gift. It has allowed me to create a collection of paintings of cityscapes entitled *Paris at Night*. I wouldn't have been able to create this collection or this book unless I believed that I could do something great. We all have these ah-ha moments. I may have more of them than you. The key, I have learned, is keeping the ah-ha moments from taking over my life.

I learned how to do this with a tool called the Wellness Recovery Action Plan written by Mary Ellen Copeland that helped me to realize how to control symptoms instead of allowing symptoms to control me. This work describes how one can rely on their own internal resources.

Medication is another tool. According to doctors, the prescription drugs Lithium and Abilify have been great friends to me. I am unsure of this. I know I heal quickly on medications, but I will always wonder what I could do without them. My quality of life is high enough on meds that I think taking them is usually but not always a good idea. It is good they are there when you just cannot be well without them.

It is also important to remember that my peers are dying twenty-five years earlier, according to a well-known report from the National Association of State Mental Health Program Directors. Sedentary lifestyles, stress, and sharp weight gains on certain medications are thought to be behind that figure.

Art carried me through times that I could not move through alone. After I started painting, I saw my own skills instead of my shortcomings. It didn't matter that I could barely put a sentence together in a logical amount of time. I had a way of communicating without words, and I began to speak a symphony of deep pain and hope. That communication led me to heal by sharing my work with others. They heard me and were excited about what I had to say. I shared my works with the Georgia Mental Health Consumer Network, and my art was posted on their Web site. The local NAMI chapter heard about me through my father and invited me to speak publicly about my art. My voice was getting louder.

I heard about the Certified Peer Specialist Project in Georgia through the Depression and Bipolar Support Alliance. I knew to be an effective leader in my community, I needed this training. This project assists people with mental health issues in learning a recovery skill set, essentially empowering them to be community leaders in wellness.

My training was nine days long. It was rigorous, and my insurance company cut off my short-term disability benefits when they heard I was there. I gained the ability to share my experience with my peers, people I had referred to as "patients" in the past. Coming from a helping profession, I found myself on a new plane of existence, one where my experience in living with a mental health issue was valued. That gave me new life, one of giving and receiving.

This book is one of the many creations that have unfolded before me. My father has said he regretted that he did not know more about how to help me earlier in life. He took it back, when I asked him if he would honestly change anything. I said I would not. In these chapters, I describe what I would not change for a moment: the growth of my gift, what some would call mental illness.

I have been told by some that they feel a need for Lithium to stabilize them after reading certain chapters due to the twists and turns. This is the path of recovery. It is far from linear. My journey continues to unfold day by day.

I write these words from all that is human inside me and warn you that this is not a professional text that espouses dry facts or consensus statements on what is different and what is "normal." Nor is this a policy document. This work is vulnerable, like the human spirit. It speaks to the life that many want to have: love, sexuality, learning, relationships, individual beliefs, and a career. This book is a mixed bag, just like life. I was tempted to remove words that I consider more risqué from this work but chose to be human instead and leave them. We all deserve to be accepted just as we are: human.

1

Pages from my Diary

March 8, 2003

Dear Diary,

I dreamt I passed an angel puking on the sidewalk. I was late to dinner with my graduate school class. We had dinner sitting on the table instead of at it.

March 9, 2003

Dear Diary,

I dreamt I got into an elevator that rose to the top of a mountain, and up there was nowhere to get off; just a cliff below. In fear, I pressed on and huddled in the back of the elevator. The elevator made it to the ground floor, and the building crew laughed about the fourth floor not being built yet.

My friend George says that when you kill a fish a chemical is released that changes the flavor. This is the reason there are fish tanks in all the restaurants and hotels in China. Also, he said he thinks artists are crazy, because they have to be crazy to be creative. He said he likes Picasso because he was crazy. Also, he likes Van Gogh and commented that he committed suicide. George added, "Are you an artist?" I said, "Yes," and he said, "Oh."

He wants me to visit Shanghai, and I may.

March 23, 2003

Dear Diary,

(For Chen)
Take all the pictures of us
Forgotten the day you buried me with your snow shovel
Take your favorite T-shirt back
Remember your abandonment in Grand Central Station
Quit smiling at me, don't wink

March 26, 2003

Dear Diary,

I've written a short piece for National Public Radio:

Carol A. Coussons has a master's degree in psychology and is a research assistant for the Department of Veterans Affairs in Augusta, Georgia. She interviews veterans with serious mental illnesses and works with a research team to devise strategies that will improve their quality of life:

Someone told me I should be happy about the war in Iraq because it means more business for me. I am not happy at all. The stress of war can do horrific things to the human mind, whether you are a soldier or a citizen. I had a friend in high school (Lorishka) who grew up in the war-torn land of Iran, and her scars from that were devastating. The war reminds me of her, and I really miss her. Unable to find her, I have written a reality-based novella about our years together to try to find her again. Currently, I am searching for a publisher. It's actually about a lot more, so I'm using a pen name. In honor of citizens like her, I may go to Atlanta for a peace rally. I believe the combined powers of the world should be able to come up with a solution that doesn't involve death. This is a poem I wrote today:

Don't always speak apple pie
Often I avoid her
Other fruits taste as sweet

Measuring olive oil
Salty tears float above
Season fish divided

Don't always speak falafel
Often I avoid his olive branch
Water and wine evaporate

Peeling charred skin
Crimson tissue stains hand
Sweet pepper heart freed

Uncle don't speak bread
Often brings knives to table
Never broke her by hand

Speaking and cooking cease
Dreams of her olive skin
Rise in the smoke of fire

In April, I plan to protest discrimination based on sex with Martha Burk here at the Augusta National golf tournament—despite the war. Although I don't agree with everything the papers say that Ms. Burk has said, a leader's words sometimes fail us. What is important to me is standing up for women, because a woman has a voice that deserves to be heard even in a time of war. I hate golf but believe a world-class club should hold world-class standards. Power shifts from the top down, and women in Augusta deserve to be up there—it's that simple to me.

April 1, 2003

Dear Diary,

I wrote this for Martha and women:

Women Rising

May be a bitch
Ain't your lap dog
Don't come on call
Ain't waitin' on scraps
Ain't beggin' for bones
Don't be pointin' me home
Ain't listen-in' massr
Got a grandmother clock
It say: tick-tock don't lie down
      tick-tock make a sound
      tick-tock look around

      see me bark loud at da' gate
      my growl make hooties' feets shake
      don't have to be pretty
      don't have to be sweet
      don't have to be gentle
      won't cross my legs
      won't wait on calls
      won't sip mint juleps
      won't curtsy or cry
      won't sit tongue-tied

      see me woman at war
      at every waking hour
      at every waking day
      power tells a woman to lie down
      power tells a woman to not sound
      power tells a woman to not eat

power tells a woman to go sleep
be your name Hootie or ESPN
this little woman ain't listen-in'

April 11, 2003

Dear Diary,

Martha is here. I went to a private meeting at large estate house and met her staff. We organized press kits for the next day. I met the Feminist Majority, and they are staying at my house tonight! I'm so proud. They are so organized and even brought private security.

Martha is brusque and seemingly powerful. She has a glowing presence. I am in awe of her for taking a small step to stand up nationally for the rights of women.

April 12, 2003

I made French toast for the Feminist Majority. They gave me this cute pink T-shirt to wear. I am also wearing the necklace that I photographed for the cover of my novella that I sent to book editors. I figured this would be a creative way to introduce the story to the press.

We listened to Martha, stanch advocate of women, for the day. The men who were standing between the press and Martha were asked to "step aside." They replied, "Once again we are asked to step aside." As they spoke, they refused to move for even her personal photographer.

State patrol officers were everywhere, watching us and typing on their computers in their patrol cars. No women officers were present.

I wondered if the judge, who decided the case about Martha wanting to stand at the front gate, was at the Master's. The KKK was welcomed at the back gate.

Martha unveiled all her surprises that she had described the night before. She had puppets of the KKK and the military. Also she had a huge blow-up pig with corporate logos all over it. She said, "While the men play, women pay." She thought the press would be interested in the theatrics, but they seemed to be more interested in her.

A member of the press asked me to clap and jump up and down, so I did. Then they asked the group to form a line and walk with their signs. It was a vain attempt to add more fuel to the small fire that included about fifty protestors.

As I handed out flyers, a member of the local paper said, "So what would you do if I don't take it? Scratch out my face?" I darted away from him without a word. How did he get a hold of the cover I designed for my novella? I sent it to several book editors, not to the press.

There was a gossip magazine reporter that kept trying to call me over to him. The look on his face told me that he knew something about me, and I couldn't speak.

Afterward we went to another estate house. This woman had rugs from Afghanistan she esteemed. We ate lunch as Martha mused a reporter from Vogue Magazine. *I secretly wondered if the reporter was from the military and not a real member of the press. Martha seemed quite convinced.*

I told Josephine, a member of the Feminist Majority, about the cover I sent to the book editors. She thought it was cool.

April 17, 2003

Dear Diary,

Last night I dreamt I was staying in a hotel nearby and that I was aroused from sleep to see from the window a crowd passing by wearing elaborate costumes from a movie.

Then later I dreamt that I was driving. I turned too sharply on a curve and plunged down an embankment into a deep green river with a swirl of yellow pollen on top. With time disappearing, I opened the car door and forced my body into the dark water. I could see a swirl of light from above.

April 18, 2003

Dear Diary,

I don't know what to do. I didn't want to hurt anyone, ever. Somebody help me! I don't know if help is on the way. I sent a message over the Internet on the JW site, but no one really knows me there. I can't call 911 because my phone won't work when I call out.

I am sane; I think I have been drugged by my coworkers. This is a violation of my rights as a citizen. In what country do we drug people who are sane without consent? I went to the ER and I was asked to sign a paper by a physician whose first name was punched out of his name tag. For several minutes, he refused to let me see the reverse side of the paper I was signing. When he finally let me look, I saw that it was a blank note page. The receptionist did not get me assistance for several hours, even when I told her there was a definite possibility I had been drugged.

Now the only evidence I have are papers that say I went to the ER and waited. For how long will I have these papers? For how long will I sit here without a phone?

2

Glancing into the Eyes of a CIA Assassin

This is a defiant act of bravery for a thirty-four-year-old woman, I think to myself. It is 2005 and one day after the anniversary of the demise of the Twin Towers in New York. I am rummaging through the old pictures and mementos to locate that issue of the *Atlanta Business Weekly* that I kept all these years. As I put my hand on the corner of the small paper, the stain of age is apparent, and my spine stiffens in terror.

Quickly, I glance at the front-page photo and look away. I snap shut the mahogany ottoman's lid, my secret hiding place. I trashed the video years ago, and this is the last piece of remaining evidence that could link me to the memories. That time seemed so banal initially, but in retrospect, it was laden with dread.

My story is so fantastic that no one would believe it was real, but I know what is real and what is not. I know the truth. In design, someone or some organization wants you to believe that I am insane. Who is that entity?

Could the answer lie in the photo some journalist snapped from the jailhouse to run with his lead story for the *Atlanta Business Weekly*? I used to fear it was the mafia that was after me and my secrets. Today I think it is a government agency. Where the answer lies, no one seems to know. When I detail this story to friends, all they can say is that I should call the American Civil Liberties Union.

I walk out to the long cement patio that encircles the back of my home to catch some of the sun's energy. Among the azure and salmon blooms of the hydrangeas and the tiny blossoms of the plum and golden butterfly bushes, I think I can bear this. It's important to feel surrounded by friends when glancing backward into darkness. I sink into a creaking, low-slung lounge chair to attempt a facsimile of relaxation.

It's not that the newspaper photo is so grotesque that I can't look upon his face, though his Asian features are anything but delicate. He didn't need to hide scars or horrifying features behind a mask or anything. Though, he surely had many masks to hide behind. Despite that, his features were not close to comely, which does not bother me. It is not the features that attract me to a man; it is the life itself—the quality of his character. I put the paper in my lap and look away.

◆   ◆   ◆

David seemed so decent when he took me away on trips. Wherever we were, he made sure I had my own private suite. Never would he assume that I would sleep in the same bed as him. Even when it came to love, he seemed so matter of fact. David offered to buy me a Honda Civic if I would be his friend. If I would agree to be his wife, he would give me a Volvo. I told him I wanted a classic Corvette, but that never seemed to fit into any picture of his.

David would always ask my advice on his business moves to sell scrap metal, and he seemed to genuinely appreciate my answers. There was a large empty office at his workplace that he suggested belonged to me if I would only be his wife. Sure, he had it all wrong, but I never added it up till the last minute. I breezed by the clues: his love for hearing bombs go off in movies with surround sound that would make the leather couch quake, his gun collection, and his story of killing a man that broke into his house. Until the newspapers hit the streets, those details were all I knew. My blindness is what is so devastating to me in this post-9/11 world.

The way I met David was so innocent. I was trying to track someone down to subpoena them, and I ran into a guy at an apartment complex. This guy I met was so simple, and all he seemed to want to do was help me. He said he worked at a food bank for poor people, and I respected that. After getting to know me a bit, this guy said he knew someone (David) that was looking for a college student to hang out with him.

He said David wanted someone to take shopping and go to dinner with him. David sounded lonely, like someone who needed a friend, and I volunteered. It didn't hurt my materialistic values one bit that he also happened to be a millionaire. So, the introduction was made.

David was so friendly. He had his peculiarities, like only eating in restaurants that had pictures on the menu, always carrying cash, and being fascinated with guns. I didn't like guns, and maybe that's why he never let me see his collection of nearly two hundred of them. He took me under his wing and tried to open up the world to me.

Everywhere we went, he tried to get me to try to get me to try new things, even if it was just the phone on the airplane. He would threaten to pay off my car loan, and I would tell him no. I was stubbornly determined to earn everything for myself, though I did let him buy me a microwave, a linen suit, and pay my first month of rent when I moved out on my own from home. He would joke with me that he could pay off my parents' home loans without getting their permission. I was determined not to allow him to take over my life like that. Something inside me said that would be the death of me and everything I was fighting for.

I was a friend to him. I told him when I thought people were using him for his money. There were so many people in his life that would demand things from him, and it seemed unfair. I would tell him not to give people anything they asked him for, but he wouldn't listen. The community seemed to really like him, and he knew many business owners.

What scares me the most, looking back on my relationship with him, is how he didn't want me to be afraid of anything. I was afraid of guns, so he set out to teach me to shoot. We would go to the shooting range, and I would target practice with a nine millimeter. I still have the shell casings from the gun. Some of them spilled into my pocket, and I kept them. Every now and then, I open my jewelry case to find them staring me in the face. Everyone at the shooting range seemed to know him.

What makes me most angry is that now he is being called a fugitive. That means one of two things: he was either really a fugitive, or he worked for the CIA. If the latter is true, I'm angry because no one lifted a finger to keep me from hanging out with the guy—not even my own therapist. Perhaps one might think that no one would have known that he worked for the CIA, but doesn't the government know that? Do they allow government agents to drag ordinary citizens around on business deals? I told my therapist that I thought he was too old to be hanging out with me and it was fishy that he was a millionaire. She treated my hesitancy as a cognitive dysfunction and talked me out of my fears.

◆   ◆   ◆

Our society is so jaded that we can not see love when it is staring us in the face. My love of her is so complicated that even I can't put it into a precise sentence. This is a small matter to me, because the truth is inside me. It radiates from my heart to everyone that knows me. I have been thrown into an arena to fight a lion, but I have no sword or shield.

Now, I am once again in this ludicrous position, I feel connected to a source of great peace. I know that this is the plan of a higher power to expose the greedy and violent underbelly of society. I feel like Gandhi, as I am starved of words and I feel full of deep understanding.

Today, I look up into the cornflower blue sky, on one of the last days of summer. There are no clouds today. There is nowhere to hide out here, I think as my eyes dart around. There are no trees, even. I breathe in deeply, relax … relax …

For two years I have been afraid to read and write, make stained glass, eat flax seeds, consume a diet high in salmon, have a low-carb diet, meditate on the *I-Ching*, or expose myself to anxiety-provoking situations. I was sure that one of these factors was what originally made me ill. I retraced my steps again and again. What caused this illness? My most salient fear was of reading and writing.

I clutch the newspaper in my lap tightly as I revel in the madness and mystery that suffocates my life of trust. This summer day seems devoid of oxygen.

No American could possibly understand my first unedited and unpublished novella that seems to be read by many around me. My story that left my hands was meant for one person, not for the masses. I have no opium for them; I am not Karl Marx.

After reading nine romance novels, one just flowed from my fingers like a current from the ocean. I was so consumed with illusion and love that I had to create something that mirrored the emotions I had choked inside my throat. In the small town of Augusta, there was no one to talk to about such things. No one seemed to understand the intensity of my emotions. Writing was the only outlet I had.

The depth of what I had to express goes far beyond the ordinary conversations of proper, small-town folk. Many of my new friends were just getting used to issues like getting along with African Americans in the community. Expressions of an intense love for a woman were out of the question in conversation. One can only absorb so much before one has to let out what is inside. I will never publish the novella because it contains so much unprotected, raw emotion.

Of those I can speak to openly about all of these details, most understand me. The doctors always seem to be imploring me to speak about anything but the real issues, the heart of the matter: a connection bound so close that nothing could ever destroy it. This love could not even be destroyed by the pirates of my words. When I sense someone has read my words, I tell them I had a nightmare that pirates were chasing me.

I am sure that Lorishka is somewhere out there. If the world would treat me like this for writing of her, they would have to be insane to think I would help them find her. What pain and indignation would they inflict upon my friend? She was my only soul mate for more than a decade; until I met my fiancée, Gabriel, recently.

◆   ◆   ◆

Lorishka took me under her wing back in high school. I was no one that anyone would pay attention to, just a shy, studious, emotionally abused child. She dressed me up in her fashionable clothes, taught me how to wear makeup, and spun my world with new wave music from artists like Siouxsie and the Banshees, the Cure, Depeche Mode, the Dead Kennedys, and the Ramones. Madonna was wearing men's suits, and we were diving into her short father's Armani suits to bask in strobe lights of the clubs that allowed under-eighteen-year-olds to walk through the doors. It was so fashionable in this scene to be gay.

Neither of us had matured enough to really be interested in acting on our sexuality. The laws of attraction and the opposite sex seemed infinitely more interesting, and at the same time we were inseparable. We became so close that we even took showers together. Our friends referred to us as each other's shadow. Though we had boyfriends, we were infinitely closer to each other than any boy. Our clique had a saying, "Boys are stupid."

While she did teach me how to carry on a decent conversation with others, the music, black clothes, the black eyeliner and red fingernails that she impressed upon me opened many doors into the hearts and minds of other youth that were struggling with the same heartaches that we were. Our lives were an expression of anger with the abuse we had suffered as children, frustration with our parents' inability to teach us about the world, and the inner creative genius that was suffocating in our restrictive environments. Wherever I went, there was a group of youth that spoke this language.

We became so skilled at expressing our outrage that we could hardly hear anything else. Alcohol and drugs walked into our lives, despite any attempt to fend them off. Ultimately, those substances opened a new language and conversations that were nothing like what we read in any literature. At the same time we opened the door to more dangerous situations and people than we had known before. We ran away together to DC and then Missouri, though we ultimately were brought home. I don't think that her heart ever had a home to return to after that.

Her parents' lives held no rules; everything around her was for the taking. She received almost everything that she could want from them with the exception of the kind of love that you can hold onto. Any discipline that they imparted upon her was cruel and inhumane; utterly lacking in teaching. And so I lost her to a symphony of drugs, power, and money in high school. When I finally collided with her years later, I was in college and she was married to someone who sold her cocaine when our friendship had last broken.

This is not to say that my life was not out of control, just tamer than the explosions in the backdrop of Lorishka's life. We were once again inseparable, but this time she seemed to be constantly pushing me to be closer to her husband. She had married the embodiment of her father, ultimately attracted to his unpredictable behavior and I could not stand him.

I managed to succeed in getting her to leave him. She made a casual attempt at attending a cocaine users' anonymous meeting. And it all blew apart with a phone call that identified her husband at another woman's home. She went back to him.

Then for two glorious weeks, we went to Paris together. Thanks to her mother, she spoke perfect French and we were welcomed wherever we went. This city, once her home, made her so happy. Despite back pain from an injury, she pushed herself outside to show me the city every day. Skipping down sidewalks, hand in hand, nothing could touch us here. I wish we had never come back to Atlanta.

We came home and her marriage began to eat at her again. She had a few therapy sessions, which seemed to help some. I began to feel unsafe around her, between her husband and the things that would happen at the nightclub they owned. Ultimately, trying to love Lorishka was tearing my heart apart. It was recommended that out of that love, I leave her. It was suggested that I was enabling her to continue down a destructive path.

Shamefully, I cried like the world was ending in front of her apartment as we parted ways. A large piece of the world truly was ending, and I will never be at peace with my decision.

◆　　◆　　◆

It is 2005, and I don't understand how a woman can just disappear from her life and her associates, even if she is with her husband. When I ran off years ago, fleeing everyone and everything—I made contact back home, and I didn't even carry a cell phone. My only prayer is that Lorishka is safe. The violent people that moved through her often tragic life must know where she is.

Today these voices from the past race through my heart and I face the truth that all this began with a terrorist, whose picture I hold in my lap. Only a terrorist could use such force to hunt down a woman that has never even owned a gun, a woman that loathes guns, and threaten her in search of answers. Only a sadist feels justified in further threatening and abusing a woman that has been beaten, abused, and raped by a violent society.

An airplane flies over and leaves a stream of smoke in the sky. Soon another follows, making another line to create a large X in the sky above me. I wonder for a moment who is above, marking my location for all to see.

I know underneath all that hate for me or what people think is me is society's fear of what I expressed in my novella. Like I said, I didn't write it for society, I wrote it for Lorishka. Now that everyone has read it, I see there is quite a list of areas in which it differs from the values of my neighbors, colleagues, and friends:

1. Expressing my deep love for a woman that borders on the romantic.

2. Highlighting the violence against women that is woven into our culture.

3. Placing a spotlight on the disempowering force that mental health has been in women's lives does not sit well with a ward full of psychiatrists.

4. Writing a tale of love for a Persian woman, like Lorishka, would not sit well with those that surrounded me then. This notion is as foreign as the word "peace" is to "war."

5. Facing men ravaged by war, daily, was so difficult. I wanted to heal them, but the wound was so infinitely deep. As a researcher, I was only to observe, and this seems so irreverent in the face of their pain and service to citizens. As I wrote this tale to relieve my own injury, I felt like an alien among these men and wondered how they could possibly ever understand how I feel.

I clench the paper that I pulled out of my ottoman with all my strength. You can think or say whatever you like about my state of mind because the truth is inside of me. No one can represent all that must change in society. I know that I am merely connected on a deep level to truth.

I look down at the newspaper clutched in my lap. Then I let go inside and read that article for the first time in years. I try to read without looking his photo in the eye. It says his name; it says both his names. It says CIA. It says federal law. It says selling bombs and automatic weapons.

I panic and look around to see if David is watching me. He isn't. I close the past by turning the paper upside down on the table. I meditate in the sunlight on all the wonderful things he did for me. It was David that told me not to go to China with those people. It was David that wanted to bring the world to my doorstep. It was David that wanted to make my dreams come true. It was David that included me in his business deals, trying to hone my leadership skills. If only I had known that David wasn't dealing scrap metal.

Today marks a day of forgiveness; of myself, for being so afraid for so many years. Somewhere inside, I hear a voice, "Today, I forgive you for not telling me that you were manufacturing weapons and selling them. I will release you for using the ordinary college student as your human shield, your cover. You are even forgiven for taking me to New Jersey to sell whatever the hell you were dealing to those mafia-looking men."

I stomp back inside the house, to my oak easel and canvas calling me from the rugged stone hearth. Immediately, I clutch for the three bold tones: gold, silver, and black. Quickly, I squeeze out a blob of each upon my wooden pallet. Grabbing a brush, I begin to release the terror written into my body.

The moisture-laden air does not acknowledge my affirmation, but I have made peace, and I let go. I let go of the trepidations that keep my voice in my throat and the sensations and visions that make me seek security wherever I go.

"While you are not the only man that has left scars in my life, you are the most haunting," I say out loud. "Namaste." My words echo through an empty house.

As I paint David's portrait, he appears from the layers of tempera paint with a large peace symbol on his forehead and a cloud of war over his head, or is that bunny ears? If only he could see it, something in me says he will. He remains my own personal terrorist. I wonder if everyone in America has their own personal terrorist. Perhaps the microphones in his office were the clue? Who actually records their business partner's conversations?

The hospital calls to find out whether I was satisfied with my recent visit while I am painting David's portrait to make peace with his specter. The intrusive questions feel like an assault, and I don't answer most of them. It is like an oppressive force calling, and I shake all over and feel the need to escape the tyranny of that place that surely isn't a hospital.

That place was pure torture, just like the last one. I don't understand how a U.S. citizen can be detained and tortured in her own country.

3

Peace

It was a warm humid summer afternoon in the suffocatingly small city of Augusta. In the two years since my year 2000 graduation from Augusta State Unversity's master's program, I had put my nose to the grindstone, taking the Graduate Record Exam and publishing research in service of the mentally ill. Additionally, I had worked hard to create what I called "a boring life," one with less drama. But I was annoyed with small town life and looking for more. I found it.

I saw an ad for salsa dancing at the old firehouse at seven p.m., lessons included. I was captivated with the notion of dancing, and I quickly pulled on my rainbow-colored dance skirt and sandals. Looking in the mirror of my mahogany wardrobe, I admired my youthful figure in a tiny white midriff-baring shirt and flared dance skirt with that tied at my hips. I spun around, filled with the spirit of life. I stopped to see my long blond tresses spinning.

Full of energy, I left to go out alone to the firehouse. I glanced at the temporary tattoo that I had carefully placed around the top of my arm. It made me think of my roommate, Meredith, who had lived with me till she had a heart attack. She had divorced herself of everything that reminded her of her illness, including me. Despite her vows of eternal friendship and devotion, she was marrying an army brat in the fall. I was so lonely without her at my side for facials, temporary tattoos, tea, and dates with medical students.

As I gazed through the firehouse's large glass doors, I could see through a crowd of glittering people to a fountain in the courtyard. As I walked into the room, an older, balding man who was collecting entrance fees looked me up and down. His gaze reminded me that I was full of youth and a free, single woman.

Inside, the crowd had gathered underneath a few sparkling lights that shone like little stars. This proud-looking, tall Asian man with large biceps was directing the crowd in the beginning steps of salsa. Hurriedly, I looked for an available partner.

An elderly gentleman volunteered, and soon I was pacing out the steps.

I was so relieved to find a man, for several women were dancing together due to a shortage of gentlemen.

"Left foot back, left foot center, right foot forward, right foot center," directed the Asian man. He worked with two blond instructors, sparkling in their sequined gowns.

The music began with its Latin rhythms, bongo drums, and trumpets, and I lost my dance partner to a woman he knew. I paced the room, and the instructor appeared to be watching me from a distance. I got a glass of *vino*, watched, and waited.

"Would you like to dance?" I looked up to see a face that looked familiar. The man's warm brown eyes twinkled above his thin Asian features.

"Yes," I responded, entranced with the knowing gaze of his eyes.

There it began. He instructed me to move to the rhythms, and somehow I did. I felt like I was failing, but I continued to move and spin and flow as he commanded, "Don't stop, just keep going. Look at my eyes, not at your feet."

His eyes looked into mine as if he could see through me. It was as if he knew all of my hopes and fears without me uttering a single word. It seemed as if he could understand how complicated it was to be me. I just danced and tried to match his stare with the knowledge that there was one truth: men adore me.

"You want to take a break?" he asked.

"I'm ready."

"What can I get you to drink?"

"Water please," I said, as we were both dripping with sweat.

We strolled out to the courtyard. There were trees in the four corners of the patio that were outlined by cement benches, shrubbery, and flowers. At the center a large fountain stood. I could hear the cascading water just above the salsa beat pouring from the dance floor.

"You should really take lessons, you know," he said.

"Lessons, that's not really me," I said, looking at him.

He was in his early twenties and I in my late twenties. I wondered if he was just trying to convert me to the cult of dancing so he could take my money. I remembered stories of women that lost all their cash on cruises and dance lessons.

"You could be really good. You could go to competitions," he said.

"That's just not really me. Don't I know you from somewhere?" I was disappointed that this knowing man had turned into a salesman.

"We were in class together," he said. "Don't you remember?"

"No."

"When I was an undergraduate, I was in a graduate class with you."

"Oh, yeah," I said. "We were supposed to have a group project, and then I dropped out."

I barely remembered him. He had seemed so meek back then. Perhaps my ego was too large to actually notice him.

"And you left me all alone, just like a woman. Let's get out of here," he said.

"I'm with you."

He drove us to the riverfront and we walked along the train tracks and the river till dawn. He dropped me off at my house and disappeared. I forgot to give him my number.

On Monday, it was chilly when I left the house, and I put on a light sweater over my sundress as I meandered to work. I passed the nurse I work with outside smoking, and waved. I disappeared into my office to finish my paper work so the rest of my day would be free. As I chipped away at the questions, the hours passed, and suddenly there was a knock on my office door. I looked up to see flowers, quickly signed, and read the card.

It said: "Missed You 33 percent."

Now I knew I was dealing with a business man, because he was rating his emotions. So, he didn't miss me fully? Should I be grateful that he missed me at all? The thought irritated me.

The bouquet was unique and included Queen Anne's Lace. How did he know I had the nickname Queen Anne? There were snapdragons, and I took those to be symbolic of him. There were hollyhocks, daisies, and little purple flowers that I couldn't name. I called the number on the card.

"Chen," I said.

"How can I be of service?"

"Thank you for the flowers. I just met you, and I …"

"I just wanted you to have something nice," he said. "What are you doing for dinner Friday?"

"I'm yours." It was the most interesting offer that I had had in months, aside from Meredith, my roommate, insisting that I didn't need a Ph.D. because she would take care of me.

The week passed in its own mundane way, and the thought of Chen gave me energy. I felt a desire to work up his interest in me to 100 percent, if only for the game of it. He inspired me to sing songs in the bathtub and during long bike rides in the woods.

Then I had the best idea! It served my deep need for drama in my life. What if I were to rent a convertible and surprise him? Surprise him how? Maybe I could dress up and pick him up in the convertible as someone else? I bet he would be intrigued beyond words.

Yes. That was it. I called and arranged for the car. Then I dialed Chen's number. From my CD player, I could hear Julie London's mellow voice taunting, "Daddy, you better get the best for me."

"Chen," I said.

"Yes."

"This is Baby, how are you, Big Daddy?" I wanted to laugh at the ridiculous notion of calling a man I hardly knew "Big Daddy," but I stuck to the sport of the seduction.

"Ummm ... Baby, tell me how hot you are," he said.

I winced as I thought about reaching through the receiver and slapping him. "You know all about it, Daddy. I'm going to pick you up at the Renaissance Waverly on Friday, okay?"

"Sure thing. Oh, by the way, call me Dr. Wa."

"Oh, oh, yes, doctor. See you Friday."

The fact that he had entered my game pleased me greatly. Now I knew I was playing with my equal. That was the most important criteria in choosing a man; more important than physical presence.

On Friday I went to the airport to rent my car. As I passed an entire row of shiny convertible mustangs, I wondered which one had my name on it. The attendant handed me the keys, and I was gone as quickly as I could sign my name. I put the top down immediately, and I pushed the gas to at least ninety on the drag by the airport runway as the sun was setting.

In this racing car, I was free for a moment. Free from everything that I feared in Atlanta that had caused me to move to Augusta. Free from my nightmares. Free from all the men I had left behind that could never get it right. As the airport runway blew by, I was in control and at peace.

My tall clod-hopper heals got almost stuck under the pedals, and I had to pull my feet back to them. Though I had on a thin, low V-neckline, floral sundress, the breeze was not chilling. It must have been at least in the mid-eighties that night. My hair flapped across my forehead in the most exhilarating manner.

It was like coming down from a warm buzz as I geared down to turn into the hotel. There was a stampede of people leaving the hotel, and I was intimidated for a moment. Then I saw him. I rose out of the car so that he could see me.

"Chen!" I waved like I was a star beckoning the planet earth into the solar system, as my rhinestone choker gleamed in the floodlights.

"Baby!"

"Want to drive, Dr. Wa?"

"You know it."

I jumped across the stick shift to give him my seat. We tore out of the hotel lot and down the Riverwatch Parkway, speeding faster than life. He looked like a god sitting next to me in his crisp white polo shirt and navy pants, so neat and perfect. His hair floated in the breeze.

"Do you want to stop?" he asked.

"What do you mean?"

"Do you want to park?"

"Out here?" I asked.

"Yeah, over there."

"Sure, but the cops patrol this road."

"Okay." He stopped on the side of the road. "You look spectacular, Baby!"

"Thanks. As do you, Dr. Wa."

He pulled my face closer with his hand under my chin and we kissed. It was one of those kisses where you just click. That is something hard to come by, because usually in the beginning there is confusion in combining two kissing styles. But our beginning moments weren't awkward. This kiss was a piece of my soul.

"We should go dancing, so the police don't spoil our party, Dr. Wa," I said.

It was too early too be all hot and heavy. Frankly, I was bored, despite his finesse. I wanted to continue with my game.

"You're right, Baby. Let's go!"

We greeted the curb in front of the jazz club with a skid. The doorman winked at me as we rushed inside a dark, smoky, candlelit room. A band, its members wearing gold suits, belted out New Orleans–style jazz. Chen guided me by the waist to a small booth in the corner of the club. We watched the older couples bounce and sway to the rhythms. Some of them were swing dancing, and I wanted to follow their lead.

"So, what do you do, Dr. Wa?" I asked.

"That's top secret."

"Really. What do you do?"

"I change peoples lives, really," he said.

"Yes. By …?"

"I specialize in penal implants."

"Really?"

"I'm proud to say so. A man can now have a forever fresh lily, tulip, or rose implanted in place of more rugged parts."

"I'm sure that serves you well." I was laughing inside at how he could come up with something so absurd, and I was intrigued for another moment.

"Yes, it does, Baby, yes, it does. Let's get on the dance floor, Baby."

Again, Chen guided me by my waist to the dance floor.

"One, two, three, rock step," he whispered in my ear.

I bounced and spun till I couldn't breathe. It was way past midnight when we stopped. I left Chen alone at the Renaissance, and I drove home to sleep. I slept just long enough so that I could drive the mustang around town before I took it back to the airport.

That night I got an e-mail:

Hi, Carol,

Hope work is going well. I have a date later tonight but would like to see you sometime soon. Perhaps I can sneak into your bed late in the night, and when you wake up, I will be there. What do you think?

Regards,

Chen

Chills went up my spine in fear and excitement. Was he daring enough to come over here in the middle of the night in the dark? The thrill of the unknown led me to continue with this game of pursuit. I wrote back:

I'll leave my door unlocked.

I unlocked the door (I lived next to the police station.) and kissed my beautiful, black, furry Labrador goodnight. Beneath a painting of a Gustav Klimt siren, I crawled into my gold and black antique brass bed. I had fallen in love with the bed from watching the movie *The Crow*. I saw it in the lover's loft and had to have it. What I really desired was to have a romantic love of my own, one that would hold on forever and ever.

In the middle of the night, the phone rang. It was Chen.

"Look under your bed," said Chen.

"What?" I glanced at the clock. It blared three a.m.

"Look under your bed."

I hung off the side of the bed and looked underneath. Athena, my black lab, began to sniff at my hair. There was a book by Jeanette Winterson.

"Why don't you read the page I've marked and meet me at Waffle House."

"Okay, Chen." Again chills went up my spine, and I was creeped out for a moment, but at the same time, I was exhilarated by the surprise. Had he really come into my house and left again, only to call me? Waking up in the middle of the night to go to Waffle House charmed me, as it reminded me of the early morning hours of my discothèque-dancing youth.

I flicked on the light and opened the book, entitled *The PowerBook*. There was a sticky note on page twenty-four that read, *"Read at your own risk."* I read the passage that poetically described male genitals as tulips. Flowers were an integral part of my persona. I grew them, my family grew them, we told stories about them, and I always loved them. I reflected on Chen's joke at the club. To combine something so fragile with male anatomy was mind-boggling for me.

I closed the book and left for the Waffle House.

Other than Chen, there was only one old man huddled over a cup of coffee in the joint. The familiar stench of grease warmly filled the air. I sat staring at Chen, wondering if he had a snapdragon in his pants.

"Do you often break into women's homes and leave romance novels under their beds?" I asked.

"Did you like it?"

"I've never heard a woman make something so sexual into poetry."

"How did you feel about it?" Chen asked.

"I found it interesting and refreshing."

"My English teacher at Augusta State University introduced me to Jeanette Winterson, and I'm a big fan. She's my girl."

Or is she? I wondered.

"My teacher said that her works are great for women to read to gain perspective on what gender means to them," he said.

In this moment, I wondered if Chen was being my friend or was being devious. Regardless of his motive, I hungered to know more about him. I finished my hash browns with cheese and raced home. A week passed, and I heard nothing from Chen.

Then Chen called and invited me to go to the local discothèque with him and a friend. I went about making my morning pancakes with a skip under my heartbeat and a smile on my face. I got out some high-heeled shoes and practiced salsa in the kitchen before I went to work.

It was another dull day of paperwork at the VA. No one came to see me, but nonetheless, I was wound up inside about the night that would come. What surprise would it hold? I don't think I saw one living person at work that day, and I left knowing I could stay out all night without anyone knowing I was tired the next day.

I had a special dress just for the occasion and couldn't help but think about it as I drove down Wrightsboro Road to pass the Sacred Heart Cultural Center. The dress was firehouse red and short with flowers that had tiny mirrors at the center of each flower.

As I crossed the bridge over the Savannah River, I could see gray herons crossing the golf course below. I made a right onto Green Street, through the historic district, and a right onto my street, Clifton Way. I stopped at my house, number 311, and pulled up the driveway.

Athena was staring at me in the most pitiful way from her large cage that encompassed almost a third of an acre. I saw that she was chewing at the fence. It looked ridiculous, these large bites taken out of the wood.

"Athena, that's bad," I said in my authoritative maternal tone and whisked her out of her prison and into the house. It would be her preference to be indoors all the time. The sun was beating in the windows in the laundry room, something that was of great fortune to the plants in the winter. As it was August, they were outside immersed in the warm summer sun and hot, sticky, humid air.

As Athena and I walked in the kitchen, I could see the black soot around the door from a grease fire when I had tried to carry a pan of burning oil outside. It was a small galley kitchen, but just big enough for a small family like us, me and Athena. I made my way into the long living room with a large mirror accenting the beige walls. At the far end, there was a love seat sofa, an ottoman, and my computer.

I sat down to find no messages. Still, I expected Chen to come over. I shuffled through the fridge and found some tuna and spinach for dinner. I loved rare tuna with soy sauce. Fish and green veggies were all I wanted to eat with all I had learned about diet and the mind at work. After I ate, I brushed my teeth and began to dress.

It was nine p.m. when the doorbell rang. I peaked through the window to see two shadows. I flipped on the light and opened the door wide.

"Chen! Hey!"

"Hello, Carol. This is George."

His friend was not quite as attractive as him, but he had a proud look about him. They both looked ready for the disco, wearing jeans and black shirts. They stood by the door as I grabbed my purse from the glass coffee table.

"Hello, George," I said.

"Hey, let's go," said Chen.

Chen clapped his hands together, and we were gone. George jumped into the back of the black Grand Am, and Chen opened my door. His hand brushed across the small of my back as I slid into the vehicle. We made our way to Lucky's.

"This place is kind of cheesy. Are you sure you want to go here?" said Chen.

"Yeah, why not? I've never been," I replied.

Under the strobe lights, we danced. I knew we looked striking together, with my blond hair and fair skin, and Chen and George's black hair and dark skin. Chen led me in salsa and swing, when the music permitted. I managed to keep up with the steps, to my surprise. Sometimes I even found the rhythm when Chen lost it.

A couple started dancing like they were making it on the dance floor, and I had to sit down. Their gyrations were too much to watch, though I realize that is what they were after.

As we sat the song out, I drank a cola to rejuvenate myself. As I sipped, people kept coming up to Chen to say hello. He seemed to know half the club. As he spoke, I could feel his hand pressing my thigh.

After dancing, we wandered down tree-lined Broad Street, and people continued to greet Chen.

"Hey Chen," one woman said.

"Hey, Lisa, how's school? What have you been up to?"

"Oh, you know, same old same old."

"She used to be my neighbor," Chen offered in my direction.

"That's great."

We window-shopped at art galleries for another block, and then:

"Hey, Chen!"

"Hey, Ron."

Well, you get the picture. He seemed to know everyone on Broad Street.

As the evening wound down, we dropped off George at his hotel. Then Chen took me home. As we sat in the driveway, we kissed with abandon.

"Why don't you come in for some tea?" I asked.

"Sure."

Chen followed me in through the laundry room to the kitchen. As I put my hand on the kettle, he grabbed my hand and pulled it toward his chest. His other hand sunk into the small of my back, and he ushered me forward. Our lips met like excited electrons, and he grabbed at my dress. Slowly and effortlessly, he pushed me toward the bedroom. As we hit the bed, I sat straight up.

"No Chen. This isn't what I want."

"Well ... what do you want?" he asked as he recovered.

"Not this."

"How can I help you?" Chen asked as he sat on the edge of the bed.

"I don't know. I just know the next time I make love it is going to be forever."

"What ... like marriage?"

"Forever."

"Well, I can't get married for five years still. I have a schedule."

"You what?" I asked.

"I wish you had gotten to know me back in college, I was so different then and I would have married you. But now I'm not going to settle down for five years."

I realized as he said this that I had no hope of winning a forever. "That's a long time," I said.

"Just remember, I'm here for your pleasure. I want you to have fun. Just think about it."

"Okay," I said.

He held me for while.

"Chen, there is something I want you to see on my computer." I took him by the hand and walked to the living room.

"You see, there is a virus or something on my computer. I've been sending home jokes and funny movies from the VA, but this one is different."

I opened the e-mail folder and showed him a picture that was actually a slide show of several pictures.

"You see these Chinese soldiers, Chen?"

"Yes. That's really strange."

"I think I know this one, the one with the gun."

"What do you mean?"

"It just seems like someone sent it to me that knows me," I said.

"I wouldn't worry about it," he said. "Erase it."

I was full of fear that David had found me after all these years. I erased the e-mail with eagerness to dissipate my memories of his weapons, the man he said he had killed, and his stories of the CIA. I trashed it, like I trashed the video tape he had given me years earlier.

"I'm going to go," Chen said. "Call me if you need anything."

I read all of Jeanette Winterson's romance novels looking for the secret to Chen's heart. I began to wonder if he had one.

While Chen and I were dating, I had the idea to write my romance novella that could end the greatest mystery of my life. I would publish it with my face on the cover and find my best friend that I had left behind years earlier. Sara, my therapist, had convinced me to leave Lorishka, but I always missed her 100 percent.

Besides, who needs a boy in your life when you have a good girlfriend?

Chen and I trained for months to prepare for a contest in Chicago to win jobs at Universal Studios in Japan. The relationship was one of healing, as all we primarily did was dance together week after week. He invited older couples from the dance studio to come out and give us tips. We sang duets together, as I grappled to tune his pitch with my limited voice training. He was so charming and at times, he seemed heartless, like when he dropped me on my head in a spin and laughed about it. We lost the contest to a room full of classically trained dancers, and he moved to Connecticut to work for a large corporation. I began to write about life to women all over the world every day on Jeanette Winterson's Web site.

4

Falling into Peaces

I leapt into bed and dove under the warm down covers quickly, as it was quite cool this spring of 2003. Oh, what a terrible night. I had spent the entire night running around trying to find a hospital to give me a drug test. I couldn't go to the Medical College of Georgia because there are people there that know me, that work with me. That hospital is closely affiliated with the Department of Veteran's Affairs, and if someone drugged me at work, they might be looking for me at MCG. I went to my regular emergency care facility, but it was closed.

My mother insisted that we must go to Doctor's Hospital. I went, although I was curious why she was so set on Doctor's. I told the doctors calmly that I hadn't slept well the previous night, and it seemed apparent that someone has drugged me.

Mother hardly helped, and we waited for hours. As I became distressed at the wait, she assured me that everyone else had needs more important than mine. But it seemed to me that the emergency room was filled with actors pretending to be ill. I could have sworn I saw my mother's face on the cover of *Time* magazine with the title: "Mom at War."

Now in my own bed, I furiously flopped back and forth, praying for sleep to come and wondering how I could prove what I suspected. The day before, as I had taken that cola, I hesitated for a moment. My co-worker had already opened it, but I trusted her more than anyone I knew. This woman was not only foreign, a trait that speaks words of comfort to me, she also knew the pain of being a crime victim. Weeks had passed as we grew to know each other by talking about our lives. Just the previous week, I had dedicated a poem to her on the Internet, secretly and anonymously, of course:

> *I know a man, who rises every morning to rape the goddess.*
> *He doesn't think she sees him, but the goddess, she is angry.*
> *He rapes her children.*
> *He rapes the earth.*

He raped her.
Her rapist proclaimed her as he raped her.

Had I upset someone or something with my words? The thought sent me up from my bed like an arrow. I stared at my face in the mirror of my makeup dresser until dawn, hoping sleep would come. It was already five a.m.

Suddenly, there was the rush of helicopters over my house. I leapt barefoot from my bed onto the cold tile floor of the bathroom to look out the window. It had a frosted glass shutter over the pane. I peered through the opening in the top. I could barely see the blades of the chopper above the trees. What was it waiting for? Was it waiting for me? Coming for me? The thunder of the blades made my heart race as I knelt on the frozen tiles.

Without warning, I began to smell an odor, quite unfamiliar. I walked from room to room, and everywhere the same odor lingered. In panic, I began shuffling through the closet for a gas mask. Who owns a gas mask, right? Well, I thought it was cool in high school, and I thought it might come in handy during the cold war. Now, I needed it. In the moonlight seeping through the window, I could see nothing. It was just an odor without a visible source. I didn't dare turn on a light. With relief, I finally got the mask over my head, and I lay on the floor, desperate for answers and frozen in fear.

My mind flashed to the words of the reporter just days earlier at the protest. I was handing out flyers for Martha Burk, and the reporter had ushered me over.

"What would you do if no one listened to you? Just scratch their faces out?"

Oh, God. I couldn't listen at the time, much less respond to the comment. There were also reporters from a gossip magazine that kept calling to me. For some reason, I just couldn't speak to them. Lying on the floor, I tried to put it out of my mind. How did they get the cover to my novella? Was this the price that I would pay for writing such a book in a small town? Did the government detest my novella so much that now I would be gassed to death in my own home? Then I remembered Athena.

"Athena! Come here," I shouted. She seemed fine as I embraced her furry black neck. I put her in the bathroom with the window open. I figured if she was okay, maybe I would be okay. I made it a couple of hours before I began to question whether the filter was working properly. I changed my mind about the safety of the situation and was beginning to question the care I was giving my dog. Was I treating her like a devise to determine whether or not I would live? Was that fair? That seemed cold and cruel.

I planned to dress and leave at once. Quickly, I took a shower. From outside the glass panel doors, I could have sworn I heard a camera crew in the front yard.

"We are shooting live here in North Augusta," I heard a reporter say. "Right now we are just outside the house."

The morning sun that was filtering through the window sent shivers up my spine. With the sun up, it would be hard to hide. And I needed to hide because something had gone very wrong. I supposed if I was a criminal suspect, the police would have knocked down my door already. And that was the essence of everything: there was no crime. This was a small town, and perhaps I had become the witch of North Augusta; someone to be taken out, quietly. I needed to run, while they thought I was dead.

Quickly, I grabbed a towel and dried off, then dropped it. I crawled on my knees to my wardrobe and grabbed the first sundress that my hand felt. Then I ushered Athena out of the bathroom. I came to the outside door and sat there for a moment.

It looked like I was alone, but I knew the police were right there. They are my neighbors. They had always been friends with me till now. All bets were off now. If they couldn't keep away a helicopter and gas, who could? My mother couldn't. My friends couldn't. I was screwed.

Together, Athena and I walked into the backyard. The helicopter had gone, and the press couldn't see me behind the privacy fence. In minutes my neighbor, Maria, opened the gate that separated our backyards and walked directly over to me.

"Carol, what are you doing out here so early in the morning? Are you okay?" Maria didn't look like herself at all. She seemed to be up to something.

"I'm fine." I backed away from her.

"Carol, are you sure you're fine? Give me a hug." She held out her arms.

"No. I can't." I walked away. It seemed that her church members were watching from her kitchen, which hung directly over my house. It seemed to me that this was a dangerous place and I had to leave. I ran and grabbed my purse and hopped with Athena into my white Honda Accord.

I drove down the driveway, then sat at the end for several minutes, waiting to see if anyone was watching. There was no one. I knew my neighbors, the police, wouldn't understand. I had told them just days earlier that I wanted to testify against Jack for things that I can barely speak of today. The police told me they couldn't do anything about that.

As I started the engine, once more, I could smell gas in the car that seemed to be coming through the air-conditioning system. I rolled the windows down. This was really a sophisticated setup. The government must have really wanted to take me down silently. I didn't know what effect the gas would have, but I knew it was better to avoid it.

The words of the morning radio talk show host from the previous morning flashed through my head: "There is a big red cross in the sky and it is going to change everything that we know of today. If you know about this, go ahead and call us and fill us in."

That afternoon, I had heard the band Coldplay on the radio as I had driven home. Their words were, "Shouldn't I pull off my head, there is a tiger waiting to be tamed." Was the tiger here already? Had he come to take me to his home? How much had he paid them to write this song? Did he see my novella and come here to take me out? Did he really work for the CIA?

As I drove down my street, I saw a dolphin hanging from the rearview mirror of a truck. It glimmered and glowed. Perhaps this was a sign that I was playing a game, like a book I had read in which the couple played with the dolphins. In *Deep Play*, the authors swim with the dolphins and play games. This had to be a sign that I was going in the right direction. As I turned toward the Department of Veteran's Affairs, I had to turn around. Right or not, I could not go back to where this all began.

The television news station was right up the street, and I drove there and sat outside, trying to decide if I should go in. I honked my horn twice to see if someone would come out. No one did. Should I bust into the building and tell them my story? I drove to the other side of the building. There were people coming out of the back of the building, lots of them. Maybe they were trying to avoid me. Had someone told them I was coming? I drove to the highway. I had to get to another city to find help. I needed some serious help.

It was rather cool with the windows down, but this seemed to be best. I was shaking in the breeze that whipped my long blonde locks into a tangle. I passed several Purdue Chicken trucks, and they seemed like a sign, like someone was calling me a chicken for leaving.

I pushed my *Monkey Liver Soup* CD into the player. The same folktale I had listened to for weeks was now talking directly to me. The fairytale told me that the doctor at work had drugged my cola because she was after my liver. I listened to the tale over and over. It taunted me as the miles flew by. Ken Corsbie, a famous Carribean folk-tale artist, had just come to Augusta State weeks earlier to teach storytelling. I admired him so. Although I was terrified, I felt confident something would come on the horizon.

I had driven hundreds of miles, shivering the entire time, and had run out of gas. I pulled into the gas station to pump my gas only to find I didn't understand the credit card machine. I stood there, cold, credit card in hand, unable to even press a key.

A woman from another lane saw me. She whisked the card out of my hand, ran it through the machine, pressed the button, and pumped. She hardly spoke. She looked Hispanic with her long dark brown hair and warm brown eyes. When she was finished, she handed me the card and shooed me back in the car with a wave of her hand. I wanted to go with her. I wasn't sure she spoke English, but surely she could help me. I looked over at her SUV as I sat down. There was a Mexican consulate tag hanging in her from the rearview mirror, and some man was driving her.

They left as I was cranking my engine. I followed them for hundreds of miles. In Virginia, they pulled behind a police car that was parked on the highway with the lights beaming; I followed and parked behind them. The police approached their car and I waited. As they drove away, the police came up to my car. I figured that the consulate had requested some help for me from the local authorities.

The rotund officer peered into my window. "Were you following this car?" he asked.

"Yes," I said. "They helped me to get gas a long while back, and I thought they could help me."

"They said you just started following them in Virginia, ma'am. What are you up to?" His face was stern and his tone deeply serious.

"I was trying to get help. I'm going to my cousin's house in Virginia."

"Get out of the car ma'am," he commanded as he opened the door. He ushered me to stand on the side of the road as he began to search the front seat of my vehicle.

"You don't have a warrant for that," I said.

He ignored me. As he went through my briefcase, I began to wonder if the police were trying to stop me from escaping my death. Was there some kind of signal out there to track me down and find me? I hadn't died in the gas, and now they were here to take me down. He walked over to me.

"I see you have a fax from the Department of Veteran's Affairs," he said. "Whose is it?"

"It's mine."

He frowned at the answer. "How do you plan to find your cousin?"

"The phonebook."

"You know they don't put addresses in phone books anymore, and we don't let just anyone into Washington. Get in my car."

Compliantly, I got in the car despite the fact that I was terrified that I had walked through death's door. I was furious that he had searched my car and then tried to make me actually believe I couldn't find my cousin in the phonebook. We made our way to a hospital. As I got out of the vehicle, I was sure he was going to walk me into the woods and shoot me in the dark. Screaming would do no good because there was no one around. Inside the door, he was met by another officer. They sat me on a couch.

"No one is here right now," one of the officers said. "This used to be a ward, but everyone moved to a new building. We'll be here till we get the okay to move you."

I wondered if he meant the okay to kill me.

As I sat there, a tall, thin, Vietnamese officer walked in the door. "Hey, George. Let's go ahead and handcuff her. They're going to follow through with it. We've got a space for her," he said.

This seemed so wrong. This thin officer jerked my hands together and handcuffed me tightly. The cold metal pulled on my wrists. I'd never get away from them with these damn things on.

"So am I arrested?" I asked.

"Uh, yeah. Yeah, you're arrested," said the thin officer.

I couldn't believe that. This seemed like such an injustice. How could a woman be arrested for driving freely on the highway and hurting no one? I also wondered why no one had read me my Miranda rights if I was under arrest. This seemed like a big act to hide something else.

"Do you know what I like best about our country?" I asked the thin police officer sitting beside me, watching me like a hawk.

"What?"

"Freedom." I began to sing the national anthem over and over. Hours later, he got the call to move me, and he transported me in the back of his vehicle to another hospital.

Inside the center, I was told to sit on a couch in a triangular atrium next to the nurses' station to wait for my turn. I felt like I was in a twisted fairytale, as everyone had on Easter bonnets. I guessed it must have been Easter.

"Would you like some breakfast?" a nurse asked, offering me some eggs.

"No. I'm not really hungry. Thanks anyway."

"The doctor should be done soon," she said.

Minutes later a doctor came to get me. He led me to a very small office. We were close together, and he began to ask me about my family history. I looked at his name tag, which said Dr. Noormorandi.

"I'm sorry, I can't really talk right now," I said curtly.

That ended our session, and I was taken to my room. I got into bed and pulled the covers over my head. As I lay there, I sensed that they were watching me from the ceiling, perhaps with infrared vision. I tossed and turned and pretended to sleep. I wanted to sleep, but who could sleep in such a bizarre place? Hours passed, and my faceless roommate (I couldn't see her from under the blanket I had over my face.) that could not stop talking to everyone that called or passed by asked if I wanted lunch.

"Yes, but I don't want to get out of bed," I said.

"I'll bring it to you. What is your name?"

"Carol Coussons."

She returned in minutes, and I threw open the covers to see a woman in her fifties with short hair frowning as she busily paced the room. I opened the Styrofoam container that she had given me to see a crepe with asparagus in the middle. It seemed the hospital staff was sending me the message: "Your ass is grass, and we know you wrote about her crepes." I couldn't eat it, but I managed to eat the fruit on the side. I pushed the tray onto the night table, and my roommate dutifully took it away.

I plunged under the thin orange cover, hungry to hide from the world. As I lay under there, I could hear my Aunt Martha and my mother outside the door. They were talking about me, and I heard the voice of a doctor from the Department of Veteran's Affairs. It was like they were broadcasting a "This Is Your Life" show outside my door. I could hear them talking about my horrible childhood.

Then I heard a woman say, "Carol, I'm a psychologist. Would you like to talk to me?"

I had nothing to say so I remained still under the covers, and the voice's footsteps left the room.

Soon I heard another woman's voice. "Carol, I'm your court-appointed attorney. Would you like to talk to me?"

"No," I said.

"I will be at this number in case you change your mind. We talk to the judge in the morning."

I remained silent under the covers. A wave of family came through the door: my mother, my aunt, and my cousin. I uncovered my face and looked at them, speechless. What were they doing in this horrible place? Were they helping these ridiculous people to imprison me? How did they get here so fast? I knew they couldn't help me. This was much too big for them.

When everyone was gone, I got out of bed to stare out the window. I looked at the kids below, playing in an Easter egg hunt. I heard someone from the door whisper, "Aww ... look, she wants to go outside." Yes, I wanted to return to freedom and find help. Help wasn't within these walls.

Somehow morning came, and I sat before the jovial, senior Hispanic judge inside the hospital. The first attorney spoke a bunch of mumbo jumbo about me following a vehicle. Then my attorney spoke: "I'm sorry, your honor. I haven't had the opportunity to speak with my client about this case and feel I need more time to prepare."

The judge turned to me. "Do you have anything to say now?"

"I'm not even sure she is a lawyer," I said. I looked over at the supposed attorney apologetically.

He thought for a minute and said, "We need to let her go."

My mother and my aunt cried, "No! Don't let her go!" They were such fools. They had no clue that these people were not trying to help me.

"Carol, we're going to take you to your room, and I will come and get you when it is time to go," said a nurse in a maternal tone.

I didn't utter a word, figuring that was the safest way to go around here. After several minutes and the rejection of two other counselors, the nurse came to take me to the door.

"Your mom and your aunt are going to take you to your car."

"What about my dog?" I panicked that they had just taken her to the pound.

"I believe they are going to take you to get her, too."

At the door, my mom and my aunt were waiting. The three of us went to get my car. It was impounded in a lot with a huge Mexican flag waving in the air next to the American flag. I was relieved to find my laptop with my novella in its memory still inside the car. I wondered if the police had read it while I sat stranded in their "hospital."

Once my aunt and mother were in their car, I followed them to where my dog was housed. From the looks of the place, it was not a kennel of any sort, just an old office. Athena came out, wagging her tail with glee. With relief, I put her back in my car. My mother tried to get me to go to my aunt's house, but I refused, as they certainly weren't capable of helping me.

As I drove away, I passed my mother at a toll booth. She shoved a fifty through my window as a last-minute effort to help me.

Traffic seemed to be trying to muscle me over to the nearest exit. Huge streams of cars simply ushered my car off the road. I exited, naturally, and came upon a chain-store pharmacy. Inside, the music seemed to be government propaganda. It was obvious the government hated me. I grabbed a hairbrush, toothbrush, and toothpaste quickly and ran out the door. If they can find you in a chain-store pharmacy, where can they not find you?

I drove through the suburbs and thought about the "hospital." What if I had talked to the doctors? Maybe they could help me after all. I drove back. The building was clearly marked like a detention center of sorts. I stepped out of my white Honda onto the lawn in front of the building. The soft grass gave under my feet. I took another step forward. Then I quickly made an about-face and got back in my car. I was sure this was some kind of legal place, not a hospital with ordinary doctors.

For some reason, my aunt had pointed out Charles de Gaulle Airport on a map to me while we waited on my car at the impound lot. I sincerely thought of flying to France for a moment, but somehow it didn't seem that it would help. Then I decided to find my cousin who came to visit me in the hospital. My mother mentioned in passing that my aunt and uncle were off to the beach, so I could go to them.

I drove to Alexandria, Virginia. As I navigated around the suburbs, I saw two dark-skinned women holding hands and smiling gaily. What would my cousin say when I showed up at her doorstep? I stopped and parked across from a YMCA, sitting in my car with my dog, wondering where to go and what to do. A woman pulled up in a station wagon. I must have looked frazzled because she looked over at me and approached my car.

"Can I help you?" she asked.

"I'm okay."

"Can I get you anything?"

"No, I'm fine."

"Are you sure? I can buy you something from the store."

"No, thank you," I said.

What kind of possible help could she be to me? I decided to head for Washington, DC. Someone there had to be able to help me. I drove straight into the heart of downtown, past the White House, down rows and rows of condos. I saw a man quickly duck into a basement apartment in an overcoat. He must work for the CIA, I thought. I paused next to a house that had a peace sign with a dove in the front. *Peace*, that was what I wanted.

I stopped at a drugstore to get a paper, a Nestle Quick, and an Almond Joy. A paperboy in a red uniform ran behind me.

"Hey!" he shouted. "Are you looking for a hotel?"

"Yes," I said.

"I know a really nice one."

"I just need a Fairfield or something like that."

"I know where you can stay at a really *nice* hotel," he said.

There was some kind of insinuation in his voice, and I shut the door to the car swiftly and locked it. I realized I was definitely in a big city.

As I drove through the city neighborhoods, I saw a woman calling to me from the driveway of a fast food place. She held her hands up and motioned from side to side inside her vehicle. I knew she was telling me that I needed to make up my mind. Would I travel to Virginia or downtown DC?

I looked ahead of me at the Virginia tags on a car. The license plate showed the hands of a child. Were the children of Virginia asking me to come to their state?

I followed the cars till it became dark and stopped at a modest motel somewhere in Virginia. I handed over my information without mentioning the dog. Surely they would kick me out if they knew about Athena. I swept myself into the room, peeking at my car from my window to make sure no one stole my laptop. I was too afraid someone would take it from me, if I brought it into the room.

There was a *Time Magazine* in the room. As I read it, it seemed that the magazine had been written for me. Yet I was not sure who knew I was here and who would print a magazine especially for me. I picked up the newspaper I had purchased just moments before. The lead story was about gay marriage. I wondered if the magazine had been planted in the store. I would have to buy my paper quicker next time, with no one around. That way they wouldn't change out the papers on me.

Morning came, and I had slept okay, considering they were watching me from the ceiling of the room. They, who? The army.

There was an International House of Pancakes on my way back to Washington, and I stopped. I had crepes with orange sauce and tried to enjoy them despite the sound of government propaganda blasting through the IHOP speakers. There were lyrics meant for me: *Since you've been gone I cannot breathe. Take me home, save me from the nothing I've become.*

As I got closer to Washington, traffic slowed to a crawl. Then I saw her in the far lane. She had a jacket over her head, and the man driving her pushed her body down as they passed me. I couldn't believe it was her. Lorishka, what were they doing to you? What were they doing to your family?

This made me more certain of where I needed to go. I needed to go to the courthouse. Obviously my novella was on trial. Had I violated some constitutional freedom? Did they believe the part about Interpol?

Downtown, I parked my car and marched into the courthouse. Someone passing me said, "Oh. You need to be in there."

Surely they meant that I was on trial, and I wasn't even there. How is that constitutional? I stumbled in and went up and down the escalators, wondering where it was that I belonged. I was totally lost, so I left. On the sidewalk, I saw a security guard.

"Hey! Can you help me?" I asked.

"What's the problem?" He smiled gently.

"Someone gassed my house and is after me."

"Well, that is an awful lot. Where are you from?"

"South Carolina."

"If I were you, I'd talk to the FBI in the J. Edgar Hoover building," he said. "They are right over there."

"Thanks!" Immediately I strolled over to the FBI, but they wouldn't let me in the door.

"Where did this happen?" asked a stern agent through a barely open door.

"South Carolina."

"You need to talk to the South Carolina FBI." She evaded my eyes as she shut the door in my face.

Feeling profoundly stupid, I decided to get back in my car. I stopped at a park with flowers and trees. I walked up to a man on a park bench. "What would you do if you needed really big help?"

"Well, I would go to the VA." He pointed to the building.

I walked over. Could they help figure out why the army was after me? As I found my body in front of the door, fear cascaded through me. These were in fact the people that I think helped drug me. I continued down the sidewalk. I asked a couple eating at a café, "What would you do if your house was gassed and no one would help you?"

"That's really terrible. Maybe talk to the firemen?"

I got back in my car and wandered till I saw a fire station. I repeated my situation to them, only to hear, "I don't know."

It seemed no one could help me in Washington. Just then I noticed a fair-haired man staring at me from his car. He walked over with a badge. "I work for the police. Can I help you?"

"Maybe."

"Why don't you follow me to the station?"

I followed him inside the station, and stood before him and his partner. They had pens poised in hand as I stood there silently.

"You know what?" I said. "I just can't do this." With a turn, I made my way back out the door. I had to leave Washington.

As I drove, I passed the Pentagon. There was an adult goose in the center lane of traffic, and I U-turned to rescue the creature. Just then I saw ten goslings. I thought of the AFLAC insurance commercials, and it seemed that someone was trying to make commercials off of me before I was even famous. Angered by that nuisance, I sped to the freeway to get out of DC.

It was growing dark, and I stopped at a Holiday Inn outside of DC. Before entering the room, I hurriedly scurried across the street to grab some ham for my dog and more chocolate milk and an Almond Joy for me. The same treatment followed me to this hotel. Someone was watching me in my room from above. I patted the bed and snuggled up to furry Athena for comfort. I slept the best I could.

When morning arrived, I decided to go to Atlanta. If I couldn't find help in DC, then maybe my therapist in Atlanta could work some miracle for me. She always had seemed to solve my problems before.

On the way to Atlanta, the highway seemed to change before my very eyes. There was all this construction, and it appeared that the army was trying to divert my travel. I pulled over in southern Virginia. As I did, I noticed an entire fleet of cars flood the city. The army appeared to be taking over, trying to prevent me from talking to anyone. I saw a police station and found a parking space.

As I walked in, a woman ran in and sat down in the chair of the front desk. It was obvious that she wasn't really a police officer. I had no choice but to get back in the car and continue what I hoped was really south. It was a leap of faith that the signs that marked the highway were real. If I headed back the way I came, that would be what they wanted. After all, the army was behind me.

In Chapel Hill, North Carolina, I found a Holiday Inn. The guy at the front desk didn't want to let me stay because of Athena, but he let me slide. I heard helicopters over the hotel, and I knew they had found me again. Perhaps my car had been bugged because I had seemed to outrun the mass of cars following me.

I took Athena to the Waffle House. She waited outside. I downed my waffle and chocolate milk. They say chocolate milk helps with Attention Deficit Disorder, and I supposedly have that. Now I had to be alert or I would die. I didn't take that medicine anymore. It made me all jittery and paranoid. I fed Athena some bacon.

When we got back to the hotel, the front desk clerk had decided to kick me out of the hotel. I knew this was a military town, and I could feel his hatred of me. Perhaps the army had informed him of the content of my novella. Or maybe it was just an order from someone of higher rank than him. As I left, I couldn't find my purse.

"Have you seen my purse?" I asked at the desk.

"No." The clerk frowned.

"It is missing, and I had it when I checked in. Did you take it?"

"No. Please get out of here." He grimaced with a look of pain and disgust.

"I'm going to call the police," I said. I was shattered at the thought of losing my only means of survival.

"Fine. Just go." He waved his arm with impatience.

I phoned the police and told them where I was as I sat in the car with Athena. Then I looked on the floorboard of the car and saw my purse. I wondered what the police would do to a woman in my situation, and I decided to split.

Upon consideration, I wasn't sure how things were going to go in the South. I decided to head up north. Maybe my friend Chen would know what was happening to me. He had seen that Chinese soldier on my computer before all this started. Maybe he was in on it. He *was* Chinese. Maybe he worked for David and knew more than he was saying.

Under the cloak of night, I sped up the highway, eager to escape this torture. On the way to Washington, I saw Route 66 and remembered when I had run away from home with Lorishka. All the boys fell madly in love with her, even my own boyfriend. Maybe I was meant to go out west. As Athena and I drove, I passed some huge trucks with FRONTIER written on the sides of the cabs. I took it as a sign that I was to find something great on the western frontier.

I pulled over to stop at a hotel and immediately saw blue lights in the back of my window. The officer approached my window.

"Ma'am, you were driving in the wrong direction on this alley."

"Oh, I didn't realize," I said.

"It's a common mistake, so just be advised. I'm going to just give you a warning." He disappeared as quickly as he had appeared.

I drove an eighth of a mile to a hotel and stopped. No sooner than Athena and I had made it to the room, there was a knock at the door. I peered through the door to see several police officers. Without choice, I opened it.

"We'd like you to come with us for a moment."

Without answering, I submitted and rode in the back of the car to the police station.

"Where are you from?" an officer asked me.

"South Carolina."

"What brings you out here?"

"I'm headed out west." He walked me down the long halls from the side door to a tiny room. It seemed obvious that he really worked for the CIA. As I sat in this little room, I watched the officers rhythmically spit chewing tobacco at lightening speed into a garbage can.

"It says in our computer that you are mentally ill," one of the officers said.

"That's not true. Do I seem ill?" A shiver went down my spine. I wondered who would say that I'm mentally ill.

"Well, what are you going to do?" the officer asked. "Just keep driving?"

"Why not?"

"What if you run out of money?" He spit another bullet of tobacco into the can. "Well, will you call someone and tell them where you are? Anyone?"

"Well ... okay," I said. "You can call my dad."

They got my dad on the phone with me.

"Honey. I want to see you." His voice was shaking.

"Okay." I knew it wouldn't help, but I really wanted to see him. And there was just the remotest chance that he could make this end.

"Will you wait till I get out there before you go anywhere else?" my dad asked.

"Yes." It was so hard to agree because the longer I waited, the more vulnerable I was.

"I have a solution," he said. "I'm going to get you out of this. Just wait for me and hear what I have to say. If you don't like it, you can carry on to wherever you're going."

"Okay." As I handed back the receiver, I had hope: this was the first human emotion other than terror and anger I had felt in days.

The police took me back to my hotel room. As I slept, I could hear the noise of different people in the next room. I heard David and his wife and became very afraid. Where they watching me to see my reaction to hearing the voice of my personal terrorist reappear in the next room? Then, suddenly, I heard *her* voice and I began to cry. I touched the wall in desperation. I wanted to go next door, but I was frozen.

The next morning, I awoke to my dad's knock at the door.

"Honey?" he called.

"Yes."

"It's great to see you," he said when I opened the door. He gave me a big hug. "Let's go have some breakfast. I brought someone I'd like you to meet. This is Jim. He was just saying that you had to be careful of the cops because they might plant drugs in your shoes."

Instantly, I worried about why this man was worried about drugs. It might be best to avoid him.

I wolfed down my waffle and ran off to the ladies' room. When I got there, I realized that the door would not lock. I began to wonder if this little side road of hotels and restaurants was a decoy just to capture people. I took a roll of toilet paper and threw it against the wall in anger. I came back to the table and announced I had to leave.

"Will you do one thing for me, Carol? It is very important," my father said.

"What?" I expected something profound.

"Will you take this calling card?" My father handed me a long-distance calling card. Instantly, I realized that someone from the phone company had put him up to this. More advertising, I said to myself. I took it and sped off. I figure out west was not the way to go and decided to travel north. Surely Chen would know what to do. He seemed to have such a mystical grip upon the universe.

I passed DC, New Jersey, and Pennsylvania. In New York, I went though a web of highways and toll booths as I looked for Connecticut. At each toll, I got new instructions from the attendant about which way to travel, as I was without a map.

Once I made it to Chen's neighborhood, I parked and left Athena in the car. I worried about her being alone. I knocked on Chen's door, and his roommate answered.

"You know, I had a friend once that thought the army was after him, and it was all in his head," he told me. His tone was so reassuring that I couldn't trust him. After all he was an actor, turned pest control man.

"Oh. Do you know when Chen will be home?"

"No."

"Can I bring my dog in and wait inside? I don't want to leave her in the car."

"No, we can't have dogs," he said.

"Well, can I sit out here and wait for Chen?"

"Sure."

As I waited, it was obvious that I was being watched by the army. They must have bugged my car after all. They were sending different women down the street to see how I would react. How entertaining Chen would find this.

It was dark. I called Chen and his voicemail each time. He never came home, never called, and I wondered what they did to him. I drove off, defeated.

It took a while to find a hotel that looked like it would take a dog in Stamford. I ended up at a Doubletree off of a nearby highway. They didn't normally take dogs but made an exception for me. In the room, I called my family to let them know where I was.

Hours later, there was a knock at the door. I looked out the peep hole to see a large woman. I opened the door to find five people standing there. One had a medical box.

"Your parents called us and thought you might need some help," said a woman at the front of this crew.

"Well, I'm not mentally ill," I proclaimed defensively.

"Why don't you just come with us and let us examine you? Then we will bring you back." Her loud tone was soothing and reassuring.

"Okay." I worried about Athena. I didn't want to lose her. On the other hand, I was sure they would send me back promptly after a few questions.

They drove me in an ambulance to the emergency room. A blonde doctor with a Yale name badge asked me what was going on. My instinct was to stay silent, but she seemed so concerned. Certainly a woman that went to Yale would have the intellect to understand my situation. Certainly she would grasp the complexity. I launched into my story.

"Someone offered me a cola that had been opened, and then I couldn't sleep. The next thing I knew, my house was gassed. I pulled a gas mask out and put it on for a while."

"You what? Oh my, you poor dear. Where did you get the gas mask?" the doctor asked.

"I bought it in high school. I thought it was cool. Then I got in my car and drove down the road. Something went wrong, though, because the army is after me. The police think I'm mentally ill, and I'm not."

"I want you to just relax. We are going to do a physical exam, so could you take off your clothes, please?"

"You're what? I don't want to take them off. Please don't make me take them off."

"Okay. Well, I'm going to take you upstairs. I want you to trust me."

As the doctor and her assistant wheeled me through the ER, they pulled a towel over my hair. I took it off to avoid being kidnapped without anyone noticing. The elevator took me to the thirteenth floor. We passed through some security doors and into a short hallway that made a T-shape with another hallway. The doctor wheeled me to the desk and handed the people behind it my purse.

"I'm going to leave you here," she said. "You should be able to go soon, so don't worry."

"What about my dog?" I asked.

"We'll take care of that."

I was taken to room number fifteen. I sat on the bed. A nurse came in and brought me a bag with the contents of my purse. She also brought me a comb, a toothbrush, and toothpaste. I put the comb to my hair and cried as I combed it. I was so touched that anyone had given me anything. Maybe this was the right place. After all, the rest of the world was hunting me down like I was a witch.

I looked out the window, and I could see fir trees as tall as the window and a highway just beyond them. The building's red bricks lined the view. With hope in my steps, I walked into the hallway. Next to my room, there was a five-foot-by-eight-foot watercolor painting of an area in Mexico, or at least it seemed that way. I wondered if whoever had captured me knew about my trip to the Baja Peninsula and how I loved those cliffs. I sat on the floor in awe of it for several minutes. I walked toward the hallway I had originally entered. I could hear people.

On the right, in the center of the hall my room was on, there was a nursing station. Behind the nurse at the window were two men in suits hunched over computers, seemingly lost to everyone else. I passed them quickly, wondering who the men in the suits were. The sound was getting louder. I heard someone singing "Happy birthday to you!" in the room ahead.

As I entered, I saw a girl with long brown hair blowing out candles. People clapped. I entered the long room and sat on a chair next to the window.

As I looked at the décor, it was obvious I was too late. There was a large bowl of flowers in the center of the room filled with wilting hollyhocks and other varieties of spring gayness. How long had they been waiting to find me?

There was an Easter bunny on the wall with different eggs that had been cut out from paper and colored. I wondered if everyone here was angry with me for taking so long to arrive. They obviously had been scavenging for me since Easter.

The room was rather dull. There were wooden chairs with orange vinyl covered cushions lining the walls and forming a gathering area around the television. On the other end of the room, there were several cafeteria-type round tables, each with four chairs. Beyond that room was a kitchen. Against the wall next to the tables were two bicycles. I knew they were for me because I couldn't live very long without a bike ride. I gazed out the window to see a sidewalk-lined street and a parking lot just beyond that. I studied the cars for a while.

At one of the tables was a lanky guy coloring pictures. I decided to be bold and sat next to him.

"Can I color?" I asked.

"Sure."

"What is that?" I asked.

He was drawing a swirl of every Crayola color available. "Shh ... just act crazy. Keep it simple," he said. He wrote *keep it simple* on his paper.

I wondered what that meant. Did he know I was hiding something? Did he mean that he acted like he was mentally ill, when he actually wasn't? Perhaps he knew David, and this was a hint to get me out of here.

The ambiguity was deafening.

I decided to leave him and the birthday girl behind and go to my room. I sat at the edge of the bed and looked out the window.

The sun was shining brightly on the large fir. The grass looked lush and soft. I wished I could just feel the grass beneath my feet. I wondered where that highway led to.

"Miss Coussons, your medicine is ready. Would you like to come to the nurses' station and take it," asked a nurse that appeared in the door.

"No. I won't be taking it," I said. "I don't need medicine."

"Well, there is a group in a few minutes. You must go to that."

I said nothing. Medicine? Who would put a person like me, in my situation, on medicine? I was the victim of a crime, not mentally ill.

There was an announcement over the speakers, "Time for group." I looked up and noticed the camera in my room for the first time.

I stumbled down the hall in the very sundress I had left my house in two weeks earlier. I noticed cameras at each end of the hall. I entered the large room again and, at the end of the room, there were more cameras. Four people sat around the television, including the lanky, brown-haired boy I had colored with. His hair was in disarray and his glasses made him look like a rocket scientist. Two youthful-looking people, a man with short brown hair and a woman with long brown hair, sat at the front of the room in golf shirts and khakis. Both were very attractive, and it seemed that I had really seen them before somewhere. It was apparent that they were leading the people in some sort of group education.

"Today we are going to talk about alternative lifestyles," said the youthful woman wearing khakis. The words the two leading the group shared meshed into a conversation on gay couples, and my eyes began to well with tears. It was apparent they had read my novella. How? It was so wrong. I raced out of the room, down the hall, and back to my room.

Inside, I cried. I wondered where Lorishka was. Did Jack put concrete shoes on her? Her business was too close to the mafia for safety's sake. I never understood how she could risk it. There was so much about her I would never understand. Was she at the bottom of a lake? Now everyone thought that I was gay because I'd written a lesbian romance novella. If only they knew my mind for marketing. If only they knew that I just wanted to know where the hell she was. This was all too much. I lay on the bed without moving. As night fell, the nurses offered dinner, and I went to the long room again.

There, I ate fried chicken with mashed potatoes and gravy. As I looked around at the other patients, I began to feel dizzy. I hadn't eaten food in days, and what the hell was in my food now? My vision became blurry.

"Ummm … does anyone else feel dizzy?" I asked.

The room was silent.

"Maybe they put LSD in the food," offered the lanky boy with all the answers.

I ran out of the room. A doctor followed. He sat next to my bed in an orange chair. "What is the problem?" he asked.

"Did they put something in the food?"

"Let's just say I'm a doctor that makes sure everyone feels okay."

"What did you put in the food? I asked. "LSD?"

"I wouldn't use LSD. If anything, I might add a sedative," admitted the doctor. Seeing he hadn't reassured me at all, he offered, "You know, some people just call me Satan." He left.

I resolved at that moment not to eat again—not here, anyway. By the time morning came, it was all clear to me. They were trying to steal my identity. That's why the men in the suits, the drugs in the food, and the stolen purse. Quickly, I grabbed the paper bag holding my things and spilled it on the bed. I picked out the most crucial pieces and hid them in my room.

"Carol, your parents are here," a nurse said from the hall.

I left my unmade bed for the first time that morning. The sun had been holding its head up for a while already.

There my parents were in the hall, waiting for me. As I kissed my mother, I noticed her hair seemed more gray than salt and pepper. She looked tired. We walked to the secured door, but she didn't leave. To the right there was a visitation room with a couple of couches and chairs with the same orange-colored plastic.

"We are so happy to see you," my father said.

"Yes," echoed Mom.

As we mumbled our hellos, I wondered when I should tell them that these people were trying to steal my identity.

The conversation rolled past my ears. I participated like a mannequin. Finally, they were beckoning the nursing staff to open the door for them to leave. As we stood in the hallway, I cupped my hand against my mother's ear.

"Mom. You have to call the FBI. They are trying to steal my identity."

She glanced at me, entirely unnerved, and ran through the doors with Dad following. Several seconds passed, yet it seemed like minutes. Suddenly two of the "patients" stood up and darted out the security door. One was the lanky boy with all the answers.

It was obvious they had caught my mother. What would they do to her? What would they do to my father? Surely they wouldn't kill her. Maybe just keep her here as a patient.

Nightfall came and the sound.

It was my doorbell. Over and over again was the sound of *my doorbell.* They had been to my house and were telling me that they knew all about me. The next thing I heard was a bunch of clicking and then voices in the hall.

"We've got it. It was in the trunk. We've got her laptop."

"What are we going to do with the car and her parents?"

"Dump them on the side of the road in the trees somewhere along the highway. Just go."

My God! They had killed my parents! What was I doing that I'd gotten my parents killed? I didn't move a muscle for fear they would come in my room and do away with me, too. My body motionless, tears began to stream down my face. In a few minutes, Satan appeared in the doorway.

He said, "What is wrong? Are you okay?"

I looked at him, wondering if he thought I would be happy they had killed my parents.

"You are evil!" I yelled at the top of my lungs.

I lay in a ball in my bed in the realization I was utterly alone, and my parents' bodies were about to be abandoned on the side of the road somewhere. I began to shake and cry, loudly, with all of my lungs. If they would stoop to this, just to steal my identity … where had I actually landed? For what seemed like the next two weeks, I stayed in bed, fasting, refusing medication, and only arising to see my "parents."

"Your parents are here," a psychology technician yelled my way.

As I made my way to the visiting room, I heard the psychology technician whisper, "Isn't it just amazing what people will do?"

"Hi, Carlie," chirped my "dad."

I looked at this man. He was much smaller than my real dad. I wanted to cry but was numb with grief. I wanted to scream, but anger didn't seem to be an emotion that could help me out of this situation. What had they promised this man? Would he steal my dad's social security or his pension while acting like my father?

"Honey, I brought you some pictures." He pulled out a laser scanner image of some photographs of our family on a thin sheet of paper. "I want you to have this." Had they already broken into the house and pulled out this artifact? Was this a sign of mercy: giving me a picture and saying goodbye, since my family is gone forever?

"*Sooo* how's the food?" asked "Mom" with the familiar rapid clip of speech.

I gazed at her in wonder. She looked so much like my own mother. Did they listen to the answering machine at the house to pick up her speech pattern? Play old family videos? Dear God, did this woman plan to go to Stateboro and play "Grandma" to my niece? Or would she just take her life savings and run? How far would this go?

"I'm not eating. I don't know," I said with wide-eyed bewilderment. Conversation was impossible; they weren't really my parents, after all. "I've got to go." I left them and trudged my way back down the hall to my room.

I did not eat.

Exactly seven sunsets later, the nurse came into the room with armaments.

"All right, Miss Coussons, it's time for some blood work," said the nurse with a twinge of anger in her voice. As I gazed into her brown eyes, I realized finally where I had seen her. She was a bartender at Jack's club in downtown Atlanta! For that matter, that was where the other familiar staff were from.

I didn't respond.

"We're going to give you medication, and you are going to eat, or we are going to put in an IV."

I was delirious with the joy of fasting and would not be able to feel the needle. It had all begun now. The golden elixir had formed. Studying the *I-Ching* for months and months, I had wondered what the *golden elixir* I had read about was. Now I knew. It was the world's hatred of me. I was so hated that my parents were killed, my identity was being stolen, and I was being forced to take antipsychotics and a mood stabilizer.

The antipsychotics would destroy my brain matter, just as they did in those postmortem studies of individuals with schizophrenia. Sure, it isn't known absolutely if the medication or the disease lead to this loss of frontal-lobe matter in those cases I read about, but I wasn't about to take any chances. The mood stabilizer would attack my liver functions. I knew the drill. This was my punishment.

What's worse, I was being played like a human soccer ball. They were offering me drugs from the same drug company from which my co-workers were trying to get a big grant. Sure, just take the pill, be our poster child. We'll sell your novella, now that your parents are dead and you're entirely alone in this world.

If I didn't take the pill, then I would be killed by Jack's employees for writing about Lorishka. I had obviously made her famous by the circulation of my unpublished novella, exposing her disappearance. What was becoming clear was that Jack may have killed her and her husband who had disappeared from the planet. I knew the message from the hospital was: choose the drug or we'll let him polish you off intravenously.

The room was spinning with the confusion of my limited choices: drugs … IV … drugs … IV … drugs … IV … drugs … IV … and I fell asleep.

The sound of a hammer forcing nails through wood woke me up. I heard one of the psychology technicians grunting and groaning. "If she doesn't, give in today I'm going to nail her to a cross!" he said. The hammering continued.

As I lay in bed thinking about my miserable situation, something came over me. I remembered a chapter in my novella. Yes! In another era of time, Jane Avril made her way out of a French asylum by dancing!

I leapt out of bed and started dancing in the hall. I waltzed with a pretend partner. I swing danced. I salsa danced with joy. On my toes, in front of the window, I tried to summon the attention of passing cars in hopes that the drivers would help me escape.

A developmentally disabled patient with short straight brown hair and clothed in long, white pajamas came out of his room and watched me. I had overheard him speaking Spanish to his family from across the hall. I grabbed his hands and began to show him the steps.

The psychology technicians and nurses were watching and began to laugh. One approached us. "I think you're getting out of here after all," he said with a big smile on his face. He had the clean cut, attractive look of a TV news reporter and was the only African American staff person in the ward.

"Okay, Miss Coussons, it's time to take your medicine," screeched the nurse down the hall.

Silent, I walked to the nurse's window in the middle of the hall. She held out a cup from the booth. I looked inside it to see a pill imprinted with the drug company name. I almost had to laugh at the ridiculous joke my friends were playing on me back home. Having the army hunt me down and drug me with their drug.

"Take it, and open your mouth so I can see," the nurse grunted.

I took it and carefully swished one of the pills under my tongue. I opened my mouth.

"Good. Now, I want you to sit in that chair right there and wait for fifteen minutes." She pointed to a reclining chair in the middle of the hall next to the phone booths in front of her.

"Okay." I sat in the chair. The pill under my tongue began to taste extremely bitter, and I felt ill. I waited and waited and finally swallowed it just to get rid of the taste.

"You can go now," she said.

I nodded my head. I felt incredibly hyper and began to skip from hall to hall. I had not seen fresh air or felt the ground in a week, and I desperately searched for an escape route.

I went to the opposite end of the hall from my room. There were four empty patient rooms with windows that didn't open. Even if they had opened, it was several stories to the ground. I went to my end of the hall and looked out. There was a street but no way to get to the ground, even if the window opened.

At least outside my room there was a tall fir tree. I could break the window and shimmy down the tree if I could reach it. In my bathroom, which only had a sink and toilet, there was a ceiling tile that looked like it could be pushed up. I could crawl through the ceiling to the staircase.

I went down the hall that formed a *T* with another corridor at the nurse's station. In the group/dining room, the ceiling tiles looked amenable to movement. Looking carefully at the ones closest to the door that led to the hall, I saw a stain. It was a dark, purplish stain. Perhaps blood, I questioned. I could crawl out the ceiling into the hall. While this was the best scenario, I decided against it. It looked like someone had tried before and, painfully, not succeeded. I looked in the visitation room. All I saw was a brick wall. I felt totally defeated and I went to my bedroom to sleep.

When I woke hours later, I decided to embrace the food, the medicine, and my "parents" to make my way out of this place through cooperation. Whatever I was up against, I was not going to allow them to drug me with an IV! I continued to dance, by myself mostly. I would take time out to draw, go to group meetings, and eat the food, which wasn't so bad. They had moved my food to the back of the tray cart to insure it wasn't tampered with. I told them I was an eyewitness against Jack, because I knew it was a federal offense to kill someone in the eyewitness protection program. It worked. The food didn't hurt me.

"Your parents are here," yelled the nurse with the long brown hair that I recognized from Jack's club. I could clearly remember her slapping up drinks on the bar in that smoky hellhole.

I was painting with a new group of patients. All the older patients had left the week before. I had to scan the laundry carts for dead bodies just to make sure they weren't polishing them off.

I honestly hated to be disturbed during painting because I loved it so much. But it looks good to be close to your family here, so I decided to see them, real or unreal.

"Hi, Mom, hi, Dad," I said without joy.

"Oh, honey, we just went to the bay. It was just gorgeous! We had dinner on the water," "Mom" said dreamily.

"Oh, and Athena is doing well. You know they don't allow dogs in that hotel, but because of you they are letting us keep her," chimed "Dad."

"We always have two of those chocolate chip cookies they make at the Doubletree because they are so good," "Mom" said. "And we went shopping at the thrift store and bought you some clothes." She pulled out a raspberry sweater and matching corduroy pants. "Don't you like those, pretty girl?"

I had instructed this woman not to buy me clothing from anywhere but the thrift store. She listened, too. I didn't want anyone here to think that I was wealthy because they would keep me till my insurance was drained to the last cent. I stared out the window.

"Did you get a mental health attorney for the trial tomorrow?" I asked.

"Not yet, dear. We just haven't had time," said "Mom."

My heart felt like it would pound out of my chest. I felt a clutching pain beneath my breast. "What do you mean you haven't found an attorney?" The pain expanded so much that I was sure I was dying. "Oh my, my chest is hurting!"

"No it's not," my "mom" said.

"Oh, it really hurts! I'm having a heart attack!"

"No, you're not," "mom" said, frowning. "Don't be silly."

"You have got to get me out of here! Do you hear me?" I demanded.

"You're fine. What are you talking about? You're just fine," said "mom."

Maybe they wanted me to die. Maybe that was part of the plan.

At the trial the next day, the judge with his dark mustache appeared before me like a Mafioso. I pled my case anyway. The court-appointed attorney who sat next to me was as worthless as his suit. My parents sat silently as the hospital manager peered down at me from above his techno-looking glasses. The brown haired psych tech smiled knowingly as he flapped his gums. I interrupted the staff's lengthy explanation of the need to extend my stay.

"Excuse me, but I have something to say."

"Yes?" asked the judge.

"Everyone here works for Jack's club," I said. "My food was being drugged till I told them I'm a federal witness against Jack. My parents brought me some dried fruit that made me feel high, so I think Jack has someone popping the lid of their trunk. I was saving these dried cherries as evidence, but I realize that I need to let go. So I threw away the evidence."

"No one has ever saved evidence before," the hospital ward manager said before jumping up and leaving the room.

"See, he had to go hide the evidence," I said. I whispered to my worthless attorney, "If I'm not out of here soon, call the FBI."

The judge sentenced me to confinement in the hospital. The days went by excruciatingly slowly. The only reprieves I had were yoga and art classes, but they were only an hour each on Monday, Wednesday, and Friday.

The group sessions led by Dr. Mayburger were like interrogation sessions: "Can anyone tell me why you're here?" Since it was May, his name seemed to symbolize a feast of our souls. Confess or stay longer was the drill.

More than anything, I needed my church, but there was none. There wasn't anything to confess, but I sure needed to lift my spirit. My spirit was dragging on the ground, and I wondered how I would ever get up after all of this. Two weeks of sunrises had passed.

I never lingered in bed, which was a sign to the staff that you weren't taking care of yourself and participating with others. At least, that is what the patients warned me. I drew pictures in the cafeteria area with magic markers.

I drew the same pictures over and over. Before my medication, my pictures were much more vivid and alive, depicting flowers and greenery. After the medication I started drawing the shapes of a dead soul over and over in deep purple, brown, and green. My brain had been sacrificed to medication. Why bother choosing a new color? I thought. I continued coloring diligently to pass the hours. I found a copy of *Dracula*, but I couldn't really read for some reason. I gave my drawings to my mother, and she liked them.

"Carol, your doctor, Dr. Generall, is here to talk to you," shouted the nurse with the long brown hair.

I entered the visitation room and saw a man with short gray hair and small round spectacles in a suit.

"So, Ms. Coussons, we meet. Why don't you have a seat?" He ushered me to a chair with an air of hospitality. "I see here from the notes that you think an army is after you."

"Yes," I said.

"Are you a member of Al Qaeda?"

I just sat there, stupefied. How could anyone think such a thing about me? I was a crime victim. My house was gassed, did he read that?! Were they now going to trash my name, too? I had dedicated the last five years of my life to helping the mentally ill, and I was not about to let them destroy that.

"I think the medication you are taking is working for you. I think we should keep it up." He tried to smile, but it was a vain effort. "I see you refused to talk to your social worker."

"I refused to speak to her when I got here, but now I can talk to her." This woman did little more than flip her curly hair around and pretend to care about the patients. I couldn't stand her.

"You need a social worker to help you plan your aftercare," the doctor said.

Yes! He did say aftercare. That meant there was a chance that I could go home. From that day on, whenever the staff asked for a show of hands for who planned to go home, I raised my hand.

"You see, Dr. Generall, I want to continue my care in Georgia with my therapist down there," I told the doctor.

"What, and move you? I don't think that we can really transport you down there."

"Why not? Why can't my parents take me?"

"I'm not sure you're ready for that kind of trip," the doctor said. "Speak to your social worker."

I was happy to think about leaving, and I went into the cafeteria. I colored, looking up only as she sat down next to me. Or should I say he? It was Jack, but he looked like a young woman. Her blond mane was more hair than he ever had. They both were quite rotund, but she had the smile of a youthful card shark. He did too, actually.

As she read the newspaper, she pointed to the ad that said, *Are you wired?* I assumed that meant she had a wire implanted in her ear. Maybe she was just someone Jack sent talk to me. Perhaps he wanted to talk me down from testifying or just wanted to make peace for killing my parents and all.

After several minutes of coloring, I had to ask: "Are you Jack?"

She nodded and said, "Yes."

Later I learned her name was Jacqueline, but I knew he had sent her here to check me out. Maybe he was even listening through a wire in her ear. We became inseparable. She was always happy and had so much in common with me. We both appreciated art. We both were planning an escape. We both hated the hospital. Jack or not, I needed a friend, and being social was a sign of health.

Jacqueline poked her head in my door. "Hey, let's go for a walk."

"Sure, let's go," I said. We began pacing from one side of the hall to the other.

"If you girls don't stop, I'm going to give you some Haldol," screeched the nurse in the hall.

"You need to leave us alone. We need exercise, and there is no place to exercise in here," Jacqueline said, sounded so authoritative that it worked. The nurse left us alone.

"I'm a photographer," said Jacque. "My photography is going to be shown soon."

"That's great!" I said.

"I just need to find a place to live. They are supposed to be helping me. I'm getting kicked out of my place because I don't pay the rent on time. My landlady is holding everything while I'm in here, though."

"That's cool."

"My girlfriend broke up with me," she said. "That's why I'm in here, because I got depressed and lost it."

"I'm sorry."

That's what we did: talked, paced the halls, ate together, went to classes, and looked at the same magazines for the 150th time. A few days later Jacque disappeared from the hospital, like everybody else. She called me for a while, but the staff made her stop. The last thing she told me was that she had become really famous. She sounded so thrilled that I had to wonder if Norwalk, Connecticut, where she lived, was the town to be in after all. With each disappearance of a new face I became hopeful and heartbroken at the same time.

I began to give up hope that they would ever let me out. Then I saw a resident. I knew his blue scrubs meant that he was going to interview someone for training purposes. I ran over to his office, before he could call anyone's name.

"So, you're a resident here?" I asked.

"Yes," he said.

"I have lots of friends who are residents back home. Could you get me out of here?"

"I can't really, uh …"

"Just tell anyone if they are looking for a wife, I will marry them if they get me out of here." This was the most desperate overture I could make.

Two weeks later another trial came. I begged my parents to get an attorney.

"Mom, Dad, we have to get an attorney, or they will never let me out of here."

"I guess you're right, dear," my mom said. "It has been a long time."

"A month!" I shouted.

"We have been calling around. Your mother called and told Dr. Generall that we wanted to take you home," said Dad in a reassuring tone. I drew in a small sigh of relief that they were agreeing to take me back to Georgia.

"You have to, you just have to," I yelped. "You've got to get a hold of Sara. They will never let me out of here if we don't call Sara." Sara was a doctor in Atlanta who I saw for depression during college.

The staff began to get wind of what was happening: my family wanted to take me and might sue to do so. The hospital judge sent a doctor to physically examine me for the second trial, but the trial never happened. They sent me home instead of waiting around for us to get an attorney.

I knew the press was waiting outside to talk to me about my book, but I saw no one as I exited the hospital. I ducked down in the back seat of the car with Athena so I wouldn't be seen. She smelled sweet from a recent bath.

All along the trip, truck drivers spotted me and radioed to other trucks. I couldn't tell if they were helping me or alerting others. I was convinced someone back home was on a witch hunt to smear my name. I was eager to go home and face them and clear my name.

All I happened to be was the author of a romance novella that got way out of hand.

We stopped to eat on the way home. I madly directed my parents to a restaurant that seemed familiar in New Jersey. I selected it out of suspicion that it was the same restaurant David had taken me to. Somehow I hoped I could find some evidence that would tell me what was happening to me. The coffee made my heart jump a beat or two, and I was sure David's men were watching me.

My mother had a coronary when I refused my meds on the way home. We went to the Medical College of Georgia, and after seeing gas come from the ceiling in my room, I found myself at Georgia Regional Hospital. I refused all food and complained that my parents had brought me to the hospital to euthanize me.

After five days, I was home again in my community, where I belonged. Who can honestly heal in a hospital?

I was ready to speak to the press at home and tell all about my novella, my missing Lorishka, and my own personal terrorist that was hunting me down. No one appeared. No one knocked on my door, not even my neighbors, the police. All was silent.

I tried to see a doctor in Augusta but was convinced he was letting the army listen to our sessions. I took on a two-hour commute to see Sara, my therapist from college. Eventually, I moved to Atlanta at her advice. It was difficult, as Jack's mafia had sent a hit man to my father's condo to scout me out. I knew that because I saw a Corvette with a plate reading: ICUDED.

5

Archangel

The winter of 2003 was the coldest one that I can remember. The world had changed forever. I moved to Atlanta out of fear for my life and being defeated by a rejection letter from the University of Georgia's counseling psychology program. I stayed close to home. Home was my dad's place because I couldn't bear to be alone. I exercised religiously, swimming and taking walks in the woods, so the Lithium and Resperidal wouldn't make me gain weight.

I hated taking my medication, but my therapist convinced me it would make me feel "safe." The medicine changed my hair, making it dry and brittle. I cut it to change my identity, and it stuck up everywhere. After I fought with it for several hours, I would look semi-human. This was difficult, as I always had been the blond bombshell, desired by the opposite sex.

After a year, I decided to escape my small world. The only reprieve I had was church and playing real estate agent for a couple of hours a day. Most of the time, I slept. I found salsa lessons at a salsa club called Sanctuary. I loved to dance and thought I could make new friends there.

"Step forward, step back. One and two, three and four. Now side to side. Right foot, left foot, turn," instructed the young, thin, brunette in a black suit.

I stumbled a bit. It had been a year since I had even thought of dance. The strobe lights of the Sanctuary were not up yet, and we danced in the warm light. Fans blew, propelling my skirt up slightly. The room was lined with mirrors and windows overlooking the parking lot ringed with boutique shops. There was a large chandelier and a staircase that went down to the entrance and another dance floor.

I turned and turned, and then we danced with partners. It was amazing to me how stiff some of the men's posture was. Just barely moving through the steps, I almost had to lead them. Whispering instructions to them, I quickly grew bored.

The lights dimmed, and the music started. I went to go sit with Christy and Charlene, friends that I had met at a Match.com party. They were plump, blond, and fun. We laughed and cooed over the boys. The conversation was gentle hum in my ear under the loud salsa rhythms.

I looked up to see a lone figure with his back against the wall. He pointed his beer to the dance floor, and I followed the lead. His dancing was amazing. His brown eyes, short brown hair, and olive skin made him look young and vibrantly handsome.

"What's your name?" I asked.

"Gabriel. What's yours?"

"Carol." I tried to keep up as his body moved with many different rhythms: one for his head, another for his shoulders, a third for his legs. It was a symphony. His dark eyes seemed so intent that I could hardly look into them. After two dances, he excused himself. Before the night was over, he came over and asked me to dance again.

"Will you meet me here next week at nine o'clock?" he asked.

"Sure!" I was so excited.

The next week, I was there and we exchanged phone numbers. After two weeks, he called me. I was at the beach with my father. The sun and seafood was healing me. Gabriel's call only made me feel stronger than I was.

When I returned to Atlanta, he invited me to go to the Havana Club in Buckhead. I walked downstairs to meet him, after I buzzed him in past the gates. A dark blue convertible Saab spun around the corner, and there he was in his sunglasses. Latin rhythms wafted from his car.

At the club, we danced closer and more together than before. We could hardly speak over the live band. As we sat during a break, he cleverly brought his face closer to mine. Our noses touched, as if he was testing to see my reaction and then his lips found mine.

That night his car broke down and we sat on the curb for hours. He insisted that I take a taxi home, but I couldn't bear to leave him. We were sipping coffee and waiting on a wrecker service when a group of men approached the car. They offered to help and with a push, we were on our way into the night.

He lived on the total opposite side of town, but that never stopped him from driving to see me after work and on the weekend. Our time together was a treasure and he never once complained about the distance.

In the days that followed, we went for long walks in the woods and swam. I cooked for him and my father. And when my father left town, I begged him to sleep beside me. He watched me take pill after pill, and somehow we managed to stay together.

◆   ◆   ◆

A year passed, and it was the end of July. Gabriel and I were passionately in love and living together. I was working for a university. I enjoyed working to uncover the secrets of domestic violence and learning how to stop it. The only real sadness was that the work made me miss Lorishka. Her husband used to push her down the stairs, break their crystal glassware, and flaunt affairs in front of her just to hurt her.

One day, I was riding on the shuttle bus from the parking lot to my office at the hospital, and I overheard the strangest conversation.

"I think those guys are just gross, sitting around and peeing on the sidewalk," said a nurse with a furrowed brow.

"Did you ever hear about Lance Armstrong and those professional bikers?" asked another nurse.

"No."

"In the Tour de France, they just go while they're riding. If they have to pee they just go, or poop, they just poop."

"Really?" the nurse asked.

"Yes. The cameras just have to shoot away real fast."

"I never knew that."

I noted this conversation. It would be healthy to share with my colleagues that seem to feel they are so far above the homeless we serve. I wondered for a moment if someone had sent them to tell this story to me. Someone like Amnesty International might have heard about me. I had been upset about my work situation for weeks. I wasn't convinced that patients were the first concern for my colleagues.

The situation got rather rough between me and my associates. Things weren't going so well at the university. I didn't like the way they were running the domestic violence study, and they decided they didn't like the way I performed my job. I was on probation for the most ridiculous things.

Then one day I interviewed a participant that had a seizure and bit his tongue. The man started spewing blood like a fountain. Next, a poor soul with HIV dropped his chewed gum on the computer I worked on. Finally, there were three nuns in the waiting room, and it seemed like someone was trying to make fun of me or try to make some type of comment to me. As if they were saying I was a martyr for caring about the participants in the study and how their rights were protected in the study. All these events during my day seemed planned.

Days later, one of my colleagues was in my office. I left and came back, and my water bottle was opened. That afternoon, I didn't drink for fear that my water was drugged. My suspicions were heightened when I saw my colleague lock her water in a drawer when she left to go across the hall.

The ER staff offered me some candy that they weren't eating, and I had a strong feeling that it was laced with something. All types of different people seemed to be lined up to look at me. Perhaps they worked for the CIA. I raced home.

On the way home, there were all these bicyclists wearing blue, and I wondered what it meant. That night it all became clear, as I saw Lance Armstrong on television.

"This is just the latest in a witch hunt," Lance Armstrong said to Larry King. He was complaining about the accusations that he had used drugs during a recent race.

Now it all made sense. The reason the bicyclists were everywhere was because the French government thought that the United States was persecuting me for writing about Lorishka. The French government was trying to signal me with these bicyclists, it was a message.

Later, I heard a story that the housing developed for the homeless in France was in bad shape and burning to the ground. This was obviously a plea for me to do something. I knew that I must give flowers to the homeless.

I went to sleep that night wondering about the helicopter over my house.

I felt like I had been beaten up when I woke. I was too weak to make breakfast. Then Gabe asked if I wanted a cola bottled in Mexico. I said please, as this was the elixir that always made me smile. But he came back from the store empty-handed because the clerk had told them the colas weren't supposed to be sold in the United States. That made me feel terrible because I love colas bottled in Mexico so much. They taste so different than colas bottled in America. They are so much more subtle and less harsh.

I stayed home that day because it was not safe to go out. No one at work expressed any concern for my well-being. I thought about going to the doctor, but I imagined that doctors don't like me very much. They were all wrapped up in the politics of the study I was working on.

I called poison control about my water being tampered with. They said go to the Emergency Department or call Quest Diagnostics, a local laboratory. I called both of them, and they said I had to have a doctor's note. So I called the Georgia Bureau of Investigations, and they said go to the police.

As I left my house, there were roofers at the house next door. I wondered if they were there to watch me. I went to the police, but the police station was closed. Outside there was a police officer helping a man with three car seats who was drinking out of a cup that said FBI. He said to me, "It's hot, and it's going to get hotter, but it's better than six feet of snow." It seemed like this man knew I was considering driving to Canada to hide at a friend's house.

I stopped at a grocery store while I was out, and a man there said to me, "I heard that there is a code red. Stay at home and don't drink any caffeinated beverages."

The checkout clerk spilled liquid on the scanner and ran my broccoli across it. I wondered what that liquid was. Then she hugged her developmentally disabled co-worker. Did she hug her to make me think she was trustable?

I called the FBI from my cell phone and told them that things were getting to be ridiculous between my water and the incident at the grocery store. They asked me my name, my education, and my phone number. They wanted to know why I thought I might be under investigation. I told them I didn't know. They asked if I had broken any laws. I said we all break laws like speeding, but I had <u>not</u> done anything illegal that could hurt anyone. As I talked to the FBI officer, all these utility vehicles around me disappeared.

"Do you see a doctor?" the officer shouted.

"What business is that of yours?" I asked.

"Next time you see your doctor, tell him I said you need to take your medication!" His tone was livid.

Frustrated with the situation, I hung up the phone.

When I came home, there were no roofers next door. I had seen an Asian man in a white van down the street when I left earlier, and when I returned he was gone. I examined the box of the granola from the grocery store carefully and threw away my broccoli.

I called my friend Margie because I thought she was speaking to my doctors. Just last week she met me at church and told me she was working for mental health services. She urged me to call my doctors. I called and left a message requesting a prescription from the doctors and called Margie back. I told her I was having trouble eating, and she insisted that I had to start eating again. She offered to bring me food and I declined, as I thought of her affinity for Steven King novels. Somehow, I believed that someone that enjoys tales of murder could not be trusted to bring me safe food. I doubted my doctors would call me back. They could be being terrorized, too.

My doctor and I had agreed that I could stop my Resperidal, but I had stopped taking Lithium on my own. I decided maybe I should start taking a bit of Lithium again. Maybe just a little would calm me down.

The next day things toned down a bit, still I was concerned. I was filled with worry for the safety of others. At the same time, it was hard for me to trust those closest to me. They seemed to be performing for others. I felt safe with my neighbors and at Costco.

I just hoped that in the home town of Martin Luther King, peace could be created.

6

War with Madness

I was headed home from the most successful day I had had in weeks, since I had been unable to return to my job studying domestic violence at the university. Despite my fear of seeing the terrorist of my mind, I pushed myself to do the seemingly impossible. I turned my cell off and drove to the American Civil Liberties Union to describe to them the fiasco that was taking place. My map guided me past Lakewood Amphitheatre to a small neighborhood, and I quickly realized I had carefully driven to the wrong place. I felt time ticking by as I made a U-turn in search of the highway.

As I breezed past construction workers building something next to the interstate entrance ramp, I became afraid that they saw me and would realize where I was going. I'm deathly afraid of utility vehicles on certain days, and if you were me, you would be too. Finally, the gold-plated capitol came into view, and the thrill of the chase ran through my body with the hope that all the mystery would end soon.

I made it downtown and scanned for the street over and over. Finally, a plump, attractive professional guided me to Farlie Street, which seemed to be really an alley. I drove back and forth trying to find address number seventy before I got out of the car. As I approached the state building for the bar association, I spied a truck blocking Farlie Street. On the side in large letters read "federal police." I didn't know whether to ask the driver where the American Civil Liberties Union was or move on, but I took it as a hint and moved on.

I drove far away to find a safe pay phone. At first I thought of the shopping center I had often gone to when I was a teen. I got there and found a large distribution center for the *Atlanta Journal and Constitution* that didn't look safe. If someone monitors the location of phone callers to the ACLU, then there's the journal waiting to pounce upon you at their signal.

So I drove toward downtown Marietta, stopping at a Mexican shopping plaza. After digging through every cubbyhole in my car, I found fifty-five cents and tossed it in a payphone quickly. My finger shook as I touched the silver buttons, dialing the ACLU. A recording came on offering the address and advising callers that no one was allowed to visit the address uninvited. Instantly, I was embarrassed that I had tried to go to the building and relieved I didn't. They gave their address to mail inquiries and the message ended.

I strolled into the store and found a Mexican Coca-Cola. My heart raced with the thrill of making contact with people that could help me and the fear that someone didn't like me, a fear compounded by recent events. I got to the counter, and the woman smiled sweetly as I awkwardly offered my limited Spanish. As I received my change, I was pleasantly surprised because the same cola costs fifty cents more on my side of town. As I left, I turned on my phone to call my friend Sophie to meet me at the square. A perfect way to explain why I am on this side of town, as I was sure the government was tracking my movements by now.

"Hey, I'm in the area," I said. "I thought I'd check out your new place."

"No way, this place is a mess," Sophie said. "We could meet for lunch. Where are you?"

"At the square."

"I've got to get dressed, but I could meet you there if I hurry. I want to miss the lunch traffic. Let's meet at Timothy's Café. Maybe we can walk, too. I really need to walk."

"Okay," I said.

I waited in the car for a while, listening to the radio. It seemed to take an eternity. Finally, I decided to risk sitting in the café. I checked to ensure my camera was attached to my purse and sighed with relief. If someone was thinking about drugging me, they would see my camera and fear identification. Once inside, I sat in a corner where I could see the sun and everyone in the room. As I waited, a blond man in his forties who was making sandwiches smiled sweetly at me, then looked away quickly. I tried to smile and only hoped it was fast enough that he saw me. There were some professional gentlemen in suits sitting in the middle of the café, talking and eating. A slow crowd trickled through, leaving with their sandwiches and sodas. Their rhythm seemed to blend with the soft rock coming from the sound system. Finally Sophie popped in the door. She was wearing a big, navy Paris T-shirt with gold letters and a drawing of the Eiffel Tower. I panicked for a moment, wondering if she had read my novella and how. It was like she was making a mockery of what represented love to me. We elbowed up to the counter.

"I'll have an egg salad sandwich on wheat," Sophie said.

"I'll have the same," I said. If they were going to put drugs in my food again, I knew that at least ordering the same thing as Sophie would make it more difficult.

As a beautiful woman with reddish-blond hair handed us our lunch, she didn't smile, and I wondered why. We sat and ate. Nothing happened. Sophie continued to yammer away and ask probing questions about my sex life with my fiancée that I avoided, as always. Her eyes glowed and her wrinkles when she smiled showed through her thick makeup. She wore lots of black eyeliner and layers of mascara. She was so young for her fifty years.

The sandwich tasted so good, I felt greedy as I cautiously ate it. As we left the restaurant, I disposed of the remainder of the sandwich in the basket before the check-out lady. She watched the basket, smiled at me, and seemed relieved. As we exited, a man walked in to meet the two men in suits sitting and talking. He looked at them expectantly, and one shook his head disappointedly. I wondered what that was about.

We exited into the bright summer sun and strolled down the sidewalk toward the square. Sophie and I breezed by the children playing at the playground and office workers sitting on benches choking down their lunches in their limited off-time. Sophie and I had all the off-time in the world, but very little was happening in our lives.

"I'm so happy that you're walking with me. I've been so lazy these days and that's just not good," Sophie said, beaming. She is slightly overweight despite working on her binge eating.

In the spirit of exercise, I followed Sophie in the high-heeled salsa shoes I was wearing. I was determined that we would accomplish a goal—any goal. We clicked past a deserted theater that looked like its ceiling would cave in at any moment, down the hill, and back up around the Baptist church my parents had taken me to when I was little. The church had seemed enormous when I was a child. It was a huge monument of stone and colored glass. Having an inspiring structure to house your Sunday rituals can seem as spiritual as the ritual itself. We grabbed two lemonades and gulped them down at a summer farmers' market next to the church. We crossed the street to window shop.

"Let's go in here," I said.

"I was just in there last week. What's next door," she asked.

There were three monkeys sitting on a bench: hear no evil, see no evil, tell no evil. The comical brass sculptures made me laugh. I said, "I want those on my front porch!"

Inside, there were towers of collectable and musty belongings. I found a $200 dingy, white rabbit fur purse that looked rather old and sickly.

"Hey, Sophie I found something for you!"

"Yeah, right," she said.

"Oh, you would be quite popular with this purse."

"I'm sure."

The shopkeeper came over. She exclaimed as she peered over her spectacles, "You should check out next door."

"I've been there already," Sophie said.

"But you haven't seen the new garden section in the back," the woman said.

"Okay," we parroted in unison before stumbling next door.

Inside, I showed Sophie a scarf that was wild with bright orange, lime green, and vanilla swirls.

"Hmmm ..." she said.

"Can I help you ladies?" asked the short, gray-haired shopkeeper in the soft tone of a woman that had walked the world for a while.

"Well, I tried to get her to buy the fur purse next door," I said.

"Oh, yes, that is truly lovely," said the shopkeeper with conviction that showed she knew about the bag.

"Yes, I told her she would be very popular with that bag."

"I agree."

"That's okay. I don't need that kind of purse," Sophie said.

The shopkeeper turned to me. "I get the feeling, darling, that you're popular and you don't want to be."

Shattered by her entrance into my thoughts, I marched back to see the garden. Sophie and I stumbled back and forth, but there was no sign of a garden. There were no flowers, no butterflies, no birds—just one cement rabbit shuffled among a cacophony of antiques and adornments. As we exited, the shopkeeper asked us to fill out a questionnaire regarding our opinion of having outdoor displays of merchandise.

I penned, "It gives the feeling of an art fair." I was remembering all the fairs in Augusta on Artist's Row.

Outside, Sophie and I parted at the square, and I escape without letting her intrude too far into my private world. Sophie claims that I am too secretive for her. On the way home, I stopped at the Spanish market to get a pound of chorizo. I felt absolutely triumphant about my progress in obtaining more food from strangers. I raced back home, filled with the joy of being out of my house by myself for two days. Without anyone's assistance, I was healing and outsmarting my fears, real or unreal.

As I drove up to the house, I saw two Gwinnett County police cars. Anxiety, panic, and anguish flooded over my body. I walked toward them as they peered into my garage.

"Can I help you?" I called across the lawn.

"Who lives here?" asked the female officer.

"My fiancée and I."

"We have been ordered by a judge to take you in for a psychological evaluation," she said.

"Why?" I asked in a pleading voice.

"I don't know why. They don't tell us that."

"Can I get my cell phone and tell someone where I'm going?" I asked.

"No."

"Can I get my purse?"

"No," the officer said.

"Can I go inside and put on some underwear?" The horror of being around people that would judge me on a cold hospital table sent the sensation of tiny lead spikes coursing through my veins.

"No." Swiftly the policewoman, with a closely shaved haircut and bright lime eye shadow, handcuffed me in front of all of the neighbors.

"I need to write a letter to the ACLU before we go because I cannot live like this. I am very worried about our country."

"I'm sorry, honey. That's just the way it is. I'm worried, too."

"Do you need assistance?" her partner asked.

"No, I'm fine." She put me in the back of her vehicle and took me to the Gwinnett Health Center. I saw a Domestic Violence Task Force sticker on the side of her partner's car.

"Are you married?" the officer asked me, peering at me in the rearview mirror with a smile in her eyes.

"No, I'm engaged."

"That's nice. Is he good to you?"

"Yes," I said.

"Do your parents like your fiancée?"

"They love him. What do you do?"

"Oh, I just push papers in the office," the officer said. "You know subpoenas and that kind of stuff."

"Are you on some type of task force?"

"No, I usually just sit in the office."

"Oh," I said, baffled that I was special enough for her to quit pushing papers for a while. I couldn't believe that the neighbors saw the police in front of my house, much less me in handcuffs. I was so full of rage at the injustice that I could be guilty of no crime and yet plucked from my world in such a brutal manner.

"I used to be married, but now I'm divorced," she said. "It was really horrible. He lost interest in me, and there was no sex. Ain't that a shame?"

"Hmm …" How and why this was important right now, I couldn't figure out. After what seemed like an eternity, we found ourselves at the medical center. The signed me in.

"Am I going to have to pay for this?" I asked.

"I don't see why you would. You didn't ask for it."

I stared blankly at the phone next to us in the waiting room as children hopped around making silly noises. A man across from me stared at my indignation as the officer removed my handcuffs. "I can't call anyone because all my phone numbers are in the cell phone," I said.

"Yeah. That's the shame of technology," she said, smiling softly as she turned the pages of an *Architectural Digest*. "Look at this," she said.

"Mm …" I was now livid and wondering how she could entertain and distract herself from the injustice before her, the injustice of her job. "What if I refuse the evaluation?"

"You don't want to do that. It won't look good," she said.

Won't look good to whom? I wondered. How could it look bad that I didn't think I needed a doctor's evaluation? I wonder who could have complained about me to a judge. I'd never hurt anyone or anything. I told people I thought something was really wrong, but I didn't hurt anyone. The air was so thick, I could have choked.

"I don't understand why they can't just send a social worker to your house to do an assessment," I said.

"That's a great idea. You should write someone."

"It sure would be a lot cheaper than sending two police cars."

"We are ready for her," the receptionist said.

Within seconds, the police officer was gone. I was taken to a room. Inside, a short, wild-eyed man with chestnut hair was biting his nails and waiting to see the doctor. There was a security guard at the door. We sat in the smallest room imaginable guarded by one of the largest men I have ever seen. The situation seemed so ridiculous. I knew my new friend and I looked rather meek. I guessed that's what people looked like when they faced the combination of doctors, insurance companies, and pharmaceutical companies in a hospital.

"Honey!" yelled the man as he saw his wife at the door. "What took you so long?"

A svelte blonde rushed in the door in a dress that looked like a country quilt.

"I'm sorry. The neighbors came over and wanted to talk. You know how they are, and I couldn't tell them. I just lost track." She smiled brightly and patted him on the knee.

"I've really done it this time. I can't believe this. All I did was say I was so angry that I could hurt someone, and here I am." He put his hand on his forehead as beads of sweat ran down his face.

"Who did you say it to?" She was still smiling.

"My doctor."

"I don't like that doctor, but why did you tell her that?"

"I thought I could trust her," he said. "This is so stupid. Now I'm going to be sent away or something. I can't believe I did this."

"They can't just send you away," I interrupted.

"They can't?" he asked.

"No, they have to have a reason, and they don't want to because it is very expensive."

"Oh." The creases in his forehead relaxed a bit, which was a relief because this sterile room was too small for extreme emotions. "What are the reasons they would?"

"I can't really tell you that, but didn't they tell you why you're here?"

"What are y'all talking about over there?" asked the security guard.

"They didn't tell him why he's here, and he's freaking out," I said.

"Oh, no one told you how things work around here?" He relaxed his posture and leaned forward with a knowing smile.

"The nurse wants you to see the doctor. The doctor is going to assess you to see if you can go home or if you have to stay for a while," said the security guard with a great deal of warmth.

"How long till we see the doctor?" the man asked.

"Probably about four hours," I moaned.

The guard looked carefully at his watch, thought awhile, and said, "Yeah. That's about right. You'll probably be here for about four hours."

I sighed, thinking how stupid it was for me to be in this confinement. I didn't feel like hurting anyone and didn't feel like hurting myself. That was the only criteria for which they could keep you, and I was sure I was going home.

Hours later, a nurse came to get me from the tiny holding chamber. I had managed to call my father and tell him I would call him to take me home soon, as I assured him that everything was okay. The nurse took me into another suffocatingly small room and drew four vials of my blood for a drug test. I was thinking silently: just hold up! Wait a minute. What the hell do you mean you are going to test me for drugs now?! For weeks I had been complaining to my doctor that I was being drugged. I had been fired her about twenty-four hours earlier, and then I had complained to her that she hadn't tested me for drugs when I called her to report each incident in which I said I was drugged. Lawsuits were all she had on her mind, I was sure.

Now I knew why that man was shaking his head in Timothy's Café on the square. I had stopped them from continuing to drug me by bringing my camera with me. They were disappointed I wouldn't enter this hospital psychotic, babbling to patients as if they were someone else. Well, if the government had given me a legal drug, I was sure that it wouldn't show on a drug test anyway because it's not illicit. And if they had given me an illicit substance, it would probably get blamed on my poor fiancée that the policewoman had been voraciously questioning me about. Maybe they were trying to produce some kind of threat to keep me from reporting what I found at my job.

"Here's a cup," the nurse said. "I need a urine sample."

"Sure."

I made my way to the minuscule bathroom, seated myself on the toilet, flushed, and stood up with an empty cup. Panic flooded my body. They were going to think that I had tried to evade their test. Slowly, I made my way back to the other room. It was painful how slowly my brain worked these days. There were two streams of thought constantly flowing through my mind, and I had to ignore one to tell myself to do something or say something.

"I just forgot to do it," I said with a smile.

"That's okay. You can try again later," she said. "I'm going to take you back to the emergency room now to see the doctor."

A new nurse met us halfway and led me to the room in the emergency department which was loud from being crowded. All the examining areas were in one room but were divided by curtains that, when I looked at them closely, I saw were covered with frowny faces.

In my square, curtained room, the nurse handed me a hospital gown and a sheet.

"This is for the top, and this is for your lap. Undress."

"Do I have to undress?" I asked.

"Yes."

"Why do I have to undress? It has nothing to do with …"

"Excuse me, but everyone has to undress."

"Excuse me, but I'm human," I roared with anger. How could someone giving a psychological evaluation ask a woman that has been raped and abused by society to give up her clothes? That was psychological rape. The last time I was in this situation, the sweet and stern blond psychiatrist with the Yale name tag let me keep my clothes on. With deep disappointment, I began to unravel my adornments: my long, flowing, body-hugging, floral, lime-green sundress and my ivory salsa shoes. I longed for the security of having underwear on my hips. Walking around without underwear is gynecologically healthy for a woman. But for me, it was also a symbol of freedom from all those men that say it is taboo to not wear underwear or a sign that you are "asking for it." That freedom is risky, though, because you could get caught in situations like this. Once my friend saved herself from a sexual assault because she happened to wear panty-hose and a body suit, combined, and she was locked up as if she had on a chastity belt. I had no such luck at the hospital.

Quickly, I covered myself in gowns and draped myself on the exam table to wait. I wondered if they were going to examine my body for scars so that I would be identifiable. You never knew when some would be a crime victim and need a quick identification check. Then the nurse returned.

"This is your number; it's your medical record number," she said. "No one will know you are here unless you tell them, not even your parents. They are here by the way, if you want to see them."

"Can you tell me why I'm here?"

"Your papers are in an envelope, and we can't open it. Only the doctor can."

"Where are my parents? Send them back," I said.

She clicked her pen on her clipboard. "Sorry, I can't bring them back till the doctor says so." She broke a smile, and I was shocked, as I hadn't seen her do this before.

In a few minutes, she brought back the drawing paper and pencils that my parents faithfully had with them.

I began to pen the only thing that felt safe to draw in front of others: flowers. I wanted to draw a rose, but I couldn't. A rose was so telling. My love would look like a thin veil if I started making red roses. And red, red is the color of anger. You think it's the color of love, but it is hard to know what a doctor will see. And if these doctors happened to have my novella, like the other doctors seemed to, I didn't want to play into their ridiculous game. Not to mention the fact that it is illegal to have copied my copyright-protected novella. I accidentally drew a red tulip. Then the curtain slipped back.

"Hi, Carol. I'm your doctor. Tell me what is going on." He had dark, curly hair and wore forest-green scrubs. He pulled his chair to the side of the exam table.

"Well, I'm afraid to go outside my house. Though I've been doing much better. I've been ill, and the last time I was ill I saw this man I used to know. I'm scared I'll see him again because I saw him in the hospital last time. You see …" I motioned with my hand for him to come close. "You see … he said he worked for the CIA." Suddenly, I could hear everyone else around me all too clearly. "Though I'm doing much better. I even left the house today."

"Okay," he said. "I think that you are going to need to stay with us for a little while."

"No. Why?" I whined like a child.

"I just think it is best for now. Your parents are here, and they can come back if you want to see them."

"Yes!" I said as I lay on the table like a cold, naked fish waiting to become an experiment.

A few minutes later, I heard someone loudly scoff, "She told you that?"

Then my parents came in. "Honey, look we brought you everything you asked for. We don't have to stay unless you want us to."

"Yeah, actually I'm in a hurry to get back to the condo to make a meeting," said Dad.

"No, stay. Please!" I almost screamed. Having them here felt like a sense of home, even if they did make lousy advocates. "No one knows why I'm here. Do you know who went before the judge?"

"No, sweetie. I don't know about that," my dad said.

"I can't imagine what I could have done. Who would complain about me. Did someone at the church complain?"

"Not that we know of, dear," said my dad.

I couldn't focus on what they were saying from that point till they left an hour later. It was just aimless babble about the terrible television that I had in my room. All that played was static, and it didn't turn off. Finally, my parents managed to unplug the beast of black and white lines before they left. When the staff brought my dinner, I managed to eat all the fruit, but I left the meat that looked appropriately mysterious. I didn't touch the cola. It just seemed a thoughtless choice when all this began with a cola. A new nurse came on shift just as my parents departed.

"Hi, I'm Jane. I'm the nightshift nurse. They should have you to your hospital room by midnight. We are trying to find you a ride. The sheriff is busy right now."

"Well, this is Bill, and I'm Alice. We're Carol's parents."

"Oh, Alice, how did you get that name?"

"My older brothers came up with it."

"Who was that? Some girl they used to beat up all the time?" asked the nurse.

"Well, we were just leaving," said my mom. I asked them to stay longer, but my father complained he had to get to a meeting. They hugged me and said their ritual good-byes and were gone.

The nurse, who had left, came back in. "Did you eat anything?"

"I ate the fruit." I was happy to report that because if you don't eat, they think you are paranoid.

She picked up the tray and opened the Styrofoam container. "Oh, my, rest in peace," she said as she dumped the container in the garbage can. "Can I get you a turkey sandwich?"

"Oh, please," I said with enthusiasm. I really didn't want to eat; I just wanted them to know I wasn't paranoid that they were poisoning me. A man peeked in my tent to see what I was doing.

As I continued to draw, he asked, "Can I see?"

"Sure."

He leaned over. "Very nice," he said.

Within a short time, I heard on the other side of the curtain, "She's drawing red flowers," in a tone that implied an obvious conclusion.

Finally, at three a.m. I was transported to the inpatient facility. I was allowed to dress, and the ambulance crew came in and guided me to the vehicle. They seemed nice as we slowly drove to the supposed inpatient facility. Then I noticed one of the people was not in uniform.

"Who do you work for?" I asked.

"The ambulance company," he said.

"What do you do?"

"Well, I own it."

"Own it? How many vehicles?"

"About six."

"Is it good business?"

"Oh, yeah, if you can keep them out working."

The uniformed woman in the back with curly hair pecked away on her laptop. "Can't you find a decent radio station?" she asked.

"Oh, you like all those brother stations," complained the driver.

"You can find something decent, and yeah, I like those brother stations," she said, smiling.

"How about this?" Michael Jackson's "Thriller" was blaring on the radio.

She looked at me and said, "You know he is Chester the molester."

I looked back in a mute state.

"Why are you here?" she asked.

"I was afraid to leave my house."

"What medications are you on?" She continued to peck away.

"Lithium."

"Why do you take that?"

"It's proscribed for bipolar disorder."

"Bipolar disorder!" she exclaimed with a wide grin, almost laughing, while Michael Jackson continued to sing loudly.

"Is that funny to you?" I said, angry that she would find my diagnosis a joke. "I'm not used to being asked about my private health information in an ambulance."

"Fine. You don't have to talk about it." She quit smiling.

When we arrived at the hospital, I stormed inside thinking about things that I wanted to say to this woman that would hopefully embarrass her as a health professional. When the public and private healthcare providers quit making the mentally ill into the criminally ill, I will have peace. That would mean stereotyping and racism would have to disappear, and I was not sure that was close on the horizon.

A staff member at the hospital told me that the man that owned the ambulance company was a sheriff's deputy. A chubby attendant led me down a dark hall.

"We should have a room for you. Everyone is asleep right now."

"Okay. Great," I chirped with all the enthusiasm I could muster. Positive and not paranoid, I had to be both of these if they were going to let me go from this inpatient facility. "Can you tell me why I'm here?" I asked.

"Sure," he said. "You mean they didn't tell you?"

"No."

"I don't know why they wouldn't. Just wait right there. I'll check the file." He came back and said, "It says that your parents went before a judge."

"It says what?! What do you mean it says my parents?"

"Surprised?" he asked.

"Yeah. I can't believe that. I asked them, and they said no. They said they had no idea." I was furious.

I sat and waited while a handful of staff members clicked case folders open and shut and pored over them carefully, billing for services and making treatment notes. Then a large, gray-haired woman approached me.

"Now I need you to go into this room over here. Were going to do a strip search."

"You're what?" I said.

"A strip search," she said with a warm, grandmotherly smile.

This was ridiculous, I thought, as I'd never taken my clothes off this much for strangers in my life. I was mortified these people would think I would carry a weapon. No one was even the slightest bit concerned with such atrocities at the last hospital I was at. I was even detained in Virginia without a strip search before my exoneration. What the hell was wrong with these people?

I followed the woman into the room, which was much larger than the tiny portals of the emergency room. There was an exam table in the middle.

"I'm going to hold this sheet here and watch you undress. Just place your clothes on the table."

I was silent as I obeyed like her dog.

"Now turn around. Okay, you can dress after I search your clothes." Piece by piece she returned the only semblance of my humanity in this room. Now that I was fully dressed after my second psychic rape, she led me to my room. "Do you have a nightgown?"

"Yes, my parents brought me one." Ownership of clothing seemed like power, the only status I could express. "Thank you," I threw in hastily.

In my room I began to change in the dark in hopes I wouldn't awake the woman next to me. Then I heard her arise with a clamor and shuffle into the bathroom.

"Blahhhhh ... ick ... blahh ... ohhh." She was puking out her lungs apparently. I lay in my bed. Then, in a short while, I heard her calling, "Tom ... Tom." I ran outside to the nurses' desk to get her help.

"Umm ... The girl in my room is sick. I think she needs help."

"Okay, sweetie, we'll be there," murmured a plump young woman writing away in her patient folder.

They never came. The puking didn't stop, and I realized that this was not a place that could even begin to help me. This was a place that did not care about patients. I walked into the hall, over to a man with a large silver earring and a huge silver satanic star on his finger.

"Can I have a different room?" I asked. "I'm not sure how I'm going to prove I don't have bipolar disorder if I can't sleep."

"Sure, umm … I'm not sure what we have. Well, we have this room here." He walked me to a room next to the nurses' station. It had no furniture except a bed, and the door had no handle from the inside.

"This is fine, thank you," I said with relief at escaping the noise of my room.

As I slept in the isolation chamber, I could hear bits and pieces of the conversations through the crack in the door. I distinctly heard a man say, "Maybe this is some kind of CIA cover up." I always heard everything, quite like a rabbit.

From the noise outside my room that was building, I could hear it was time to get up, although I wasn't quite sure I had slept. The door to the room was not shut tight and I walked out of my room into a scene that seemed to surely be a joke. Everyone was in their pajamas, and many of the people looked like they were just not exactly from my neighborhood, so to speak. They seemed not to be middle class but poor, but appearances rarely tell the whole story. I had nothing against differences, in fact I loved them, but waking up to a room full of strangers made me feel differently. It was as if I got stuck in the wrong bar, and no one went home. This surely was a joke. This couldn't be a hospital.

Quickly, I stepped past the patients and went to my original room to get dressed. Luckily, my young, twenty-something, toilet-hugging roommate was gone. A moment of privacy for dressing was a rare privilege in a hospital. Instead of balancing on a thin moist towel on the bathroom floor in the bathroom, I could sit on the edge of the bed. I had carefully instructed my parents to bring professional-looking clothes so that people could see that I cared about my appearance. I wanted everyone to know I had not lost my social skills. But my parents had forgotten my shoes. I clicked back into the main lobby in my salsa shoes.

I passed a rotund man in a comfortable-looking blue plaid shirt. As we passed, he whispered, "Oh, you're going home, darling. You're going home." I wasn't sure if he was flirting or not, but I was elated that I was seemingly pulling off a wake-up call in the hospital without incident.

"Coussons, is that you?" A thin man peered at me over his glasses and beckoned me forward with a smile.

"Yes."

"Come here, I want to get your vitals." He patted the chair next to him.

Looking around at the staff, I noticed they were mostly African American, while the patients were mostly Caucasian. Politically, I thought this was in my favor, as I felt persecuted for suggesting we hire an African American at my job. There was the off chance that there was a feeling of reverse racism among the staff, but I felt I could handle that, too, as I felt that was usually a reaction to per-ceived racism by the other party. Showing the opposite often put that fire out.

The man took my temperature and vital signs. "Now you can go to the cafete-ria. Oh, wait, you're not voluntary are you?"

"No."

"Just wait here. You'll be eating in here."

"Okay, thanks."

I knew this game like the back of my hand. There were two classes of people in a psychiatric unit: those that complied and those that didn't. Those that com-plied had privileges and those that didn't did not receive those bonuses. It was a system that I've always found quite discriminatory: no doctor, no medicine equals less than human.

Eventually our breakfast came. It was soggy eggs, grits, and toast; simple enough to be edible. After dining, I fell back in my chair and wondered for a moment if I should have gotten out of bed at all. I took another glass of breakfast punch and returned to my room to lie on the bed. Almost as soon as I laid my body down on the thin, dull gray comforter, I got back up because I would never get out of here if I was not social, no matter how I slept. As I walked, I felt woozy and considered whether the feeling was from more than sleep deprivation.

In the first morning group, I realized it probably was more than lack of sleep. We spoke over the symphony of three patients snoring. I was too tired to talk, and everything I heard sounded like bullshit. I would give you more detail, but I'm trying to write HIPPA compliantly. HIPPA is a government rule set regard-ing the privacy. All the patients you hear about or have heard about are imagi-nary, while my experience is completely true.

During the group I came upon an epiphany when a woman begged to be released because her insurance didn't cover hospitalization: this was all about money. Everyone, including staff, reassured her that her release was soon to take place. Just minutes before, this woman had been complaining to me rather loudly. She thought an obese staff member was a vile creature trying to overtake her. Earlier she had run down the hall to try to bust through an open door to escape. Of course, she didn't make it that time.

I left that group to be stuck on the ward with nothing to do. Patients couldn't leave the ward for other recreational groups until they complied with medication and signed up to be voluntary. Until then, I was no one. So, I drew and drew. There was a porch that led to a garden with the most beautiful flowers I had seen in a while. Of course the gate to the garden was locked tight. Still, being near flowers was inspiring.

The sun would hit me at certain times of the day, and it was like rays of energy were healing me inside. I would put my fingers through the squares of the fence and grasp a branch of a white butterfly bush. That way, I felt like I was outside and not stuck in a cage. While I was out there, I told a charismatic brunette that the food had sedatives in it. I actually ratted to whomever I could about how much I disliked my situation. The combination of confinement, pharmaceutical companies, insurance companies, and the hospital agenda came roaring through my head so fast that I ran to the phone.

As I picked up the receiver, a patient implored, "You can have privacy down the hall."

"No. I want people to hear me," I told him. Into the phone, I said, "Dad, it's me.

"Hi, honey. I was just thinking about you."

"Dad, you've got to get me out of here. Do you realize what this place is?"

"No, darling."

"Dad, this place is not about therapy. This place is about social control."

Patients could hear me and began to chant, "Yeah, that's right!" in the background.

"I need your help."

"Do you realize that I was picked up at my house by the police in front of all the neighbors?"

"No, dear," he said.

"Do you realize that I was handcuffed and taken in a police car to the hospital?"

"No."

"Have I done something wrong?"

"No."

"Do I deserve to be treated like a criminal?"

"No."

"Dad, you have to get me out of here. You failed me as a child, but this is your chance. I need you to help me. You have to get me out of here. You need to go before that judge and tell them you made a mistake. The only way they can hold me is if I'm a danger to myself or others, and I'm neither."

"Okay, Carol. I'll help."

"How could you lie to me?"

"I didn't lie to you darling."

"You said you didn't know how this happened."

"You asked how this happened, not what we said to the judge, darling. Those are two different things."

Staff began to call us for lunch and take the cords off the phone. They removed the cords so no one would strangle themselves. "Okay, Dad, I have to go, but you have to help. I love you." That was so difficult to utter, I was livid.

"I love you too, Carol, and ..."

I hung up before he could say anything else. I didn't want to hear any more. Once again I was stranded in here, left to depend on my parents that didn't understand a damn thing about mental health, the law, insurance companies, pharmaceutical companies, hospital agendas, and patriarchy that claims I am ill while the masses continue to be violent and commit crimes that make me ill.

Five days later, I was released from my captivity. The litany of group messages were spinning in my head, but one from a militant staff member offended me most: *You will always be on medication.* I had fought hard for my release. The *only* good thing that came from the hospitalization was that my doctor put me on a new, atypical antipsychotic of my choosing in addition to my Lithium.

7

Our American Dream

"Carol, your dad is on the phone," Gabriel called.

"Hey, Carol. We just picked up your dress from the cleaners and are going to come over," my father chirped loudly.

"You're what?! My dress can't sit in the car. Remember, you said you'd hang it up. You said you'd get something to hang it!" I couldn't believe he would forget what I told him.

"I didn't get anything to hang it," he said.

"I can't depend on you. Come get me now!"

"Huntley and I are on the way." Huntley was my friend I had met while attending a training to become a Certified Peer Specialist last year in 2005, which is training program that teaches a recovery skill set to individuals with mental health issues. This training enables them to mentor others with these skills.

"Good." I didn't really want to leave the house, but I had to take care of this.

At least Dad had managed to get my friend Huntley! Huntley was the key to the whole ceremony going forward without a hitch. He was going to arrange the centerpieces the next day and be on the phone for the caterers to make sure they found the reception while we were tying the knot.

It seemed like forever. I was in a panic to hang that dress before it wrinkled. I wanted the next day to be perfect.

Summer had mostly passed, but September was as warm as ever. We managed to make it to the hotel. It took two of us to carry the dress up the stairs. Underneath the clear plastic, I could see the stitched and beaded flowers around the strapless neck line. The train, my favorite part of the dress, was hidden in folds of the dress. It was a cascade of fabric accented by small, ivory, cloth roses.

Dad took the ironing board in his room and balanced the bottom of board on top of the luggage rack. The top of the ironing board leaned against the wall. He clicked the hanger on top of the ironing board, which was leaning against the wall, and he motioned for me to approve.

"You could step on my dress when you go to your suitcase, and it's leaning on that side. The hem is bent," I said. I gave it a little nudge and the balancing act collapsed. I lunged to catch it, before it hit the floor and glared at my father. Huntley patiently stared at us and didn't utter a word.

Several configurations of the ironing board and luggage rack later, I was ready to give up. Then it hit me: put the ironing board inside the dress! I moved to quickly lift the board into the dress. Suddenly there was life to the gown. We rested the bust against the wall, and the skirt opened around the luggage rack, making a perfect duo.

"I sure am glad you figured that out, sweetheart." Dad sounded relieved.

"Me too!" I was rather pleased with myself.

Huntley, Dad, and I went to dinner, and then they dropped me off at the house.

I imagine most women go out drinking with their girlfriends the night before they tie the knot. Not for me. All night I had been creating flower arrangements for the wedding with family watching in the wings. Red roses for Gabriel, my father, and his brothers, with a fern leaf, of course. To signify my groom's personal corsage, I placed a stem of some feathery green-colored plant. With the careful coaching of Gabriel's aunt, I spun floral tape and placed each in an open Ziploc bag in the fridge.

The pieces for my mother and Gabriel's mother and sister had white orchids with eucalyptus leaves. My sister's was more colorful, with fluffy purple flowers to match her purple dress. They got the same treatment as the others, with the addition of a special bow.

When I had seen a lone bouquet of white hydrangeas earlier at the market, I knew they were what I wanted. They were simple and elegant and, with white roses, perfect. The creation was quite heavy, and I bound it in wire and then wrapped the stems in a dark, sheer, antique green ribbon. The bouquet was too big for a Ziploc, so I placed them in water in a large glass vase.

Gabriel and his family were merrily drinking tequila and chattering in Spanish. His brothers and sisters were so happy to be together, a treat that comes rarely for them. After saying goodnight, I went to sleep listening to their laughter.

◆   ◆   ◆

It had been just like any other night at the Tongue and Groove. We had our dance lesson with Julian and began to spin to the salsa rhythms that drove us out of the suburbs and into the city, time and time again. The strobe lights danced off of our skin. My black, Spanish, Bebe dress opened at the side with several lengths of cloth cascading downward. When I spun, it felt like a piece of magic. When I looked into Gabriel's eyes, he was the man I had met nearly two years earlier: crisp, clean, and full of life.

We moved to the side to have a drink and cool down for a moment. As I sipped at my Coca-Cola, he put down his beer and reached into his pocket. Quickly, he placed a velvety box in my hand.

◆   ◆   ◆

"Yes!" I shouted over the Latin rhythms into his ear. I flipped it open and placed the diamond ring on my finger. As we embraced, I felt him closer to my body than ever before. Something changed in that instant, and I knew he was a part of me that I could never let go.

◆   ◆   ◆

I imagine that many brides would be irritated if they couldn't understand their spouse's family, but I had learned a few phrases, like *mucho gusto*. The look on their faces let me know that I was in a place of love. The lack of understanding was something I was used to, as I grew up around French and Dutch languages that are still foreign to me.

Morning came, and Dad came to pick me up to get ready for the day. I went to my parents' hotel and dressed. On the way to the chapel, I realized I had left my big bouquet in the room. Luckily, my mom had driven her car, and she whisked back to the room and picked it up without us missing a single photo opportunity.

The service was small, with forty family members and friends. It was conducted in both English and Spanish. As our vows began, the preacher stopped and asked Gabriel not to look at him. Gabe laughed and refocused his serious gaze upon my eyes as we promised to live together forever.

The reception was astounding. There were eighty people, and the food from Publix grocery store seemed as though it had come from some grand caterer and overflowed the tables. As we entered the hall, our guests greeted us with hugs and kisses.

In the background, there was the soft shimmer of jazz music. The band at my church, Atlanta Unity, had graciously agreed to play for a mere song, so to speak.

Huntley's centerpieces were breathtaking. There was a circular mound of roses dancing around a candle at each table. Huntley's shirt dripped in sweat, and I begged him to sit down and drink some ice water. As he conceded, he sat next to my husband's cousin from Chicago that reminds us of Shakira. They talked through the entire reception.

My parents seemed so proud and had so much fun. I was so happy to see almost my entire family there. I thought none of them would come. I thought that the stigma of all the hospitals would be too much for them to overlook. I was wrong.

As we cut the cake and delicately fed each other a square of cake, a call arose from the crowd. "*Beso, beso.*" Graciously, we complied and put our lips together. That was the best strawberry *tres leches* cake I have ever tasted.

Later, I opened presents at our house in a room of thirty of my husband's family members. His mother had magically fed everyone beans and rice, though there was almost no food in our home. There was so much joy and laughter in the room as everyone bet on how many kids we would have. In rough English, Gabriel's sister called out, "So, Carol, do you like your mattress?"

"Yes," I said, oblivious to her point.

I was so worried I wouldn't have enough wine at the reception, and we still have a full wine cooler six months later. And I miss my dress, as it found its proper home at the local Goodwill.

8

The Phone Call

My friend that got me this research job assures me that this great tree outside my window will be full of drunken birds in the spring because the fruit ripens and ferments. It is 2006 and the leaves outside are turning to duller colors than the former lush green. Now there are no brilliant yellows or oranges.

In contrast, the inside of the laboratory is sterile from my mopping the black countertops with germicide. The hood is dirty, because I just don't have the desire to clean it yet. If I never touched it again, I would be happy. The Coulter counter for counting blood cells needs priming, and I pray I never have to count another cell.

I don't think I'll make it till spring. I think that hurling myself from the third floor is more inviting than staying till spring. This is why I will move on soon, because it is unacceptable for a newlywed to be having such thoughts. Also, I am too educated about listening to the signs that articulate my needs to let this continue.

The door at the end of the laboratory opens. "There's a PK-B out here!" The door shuts and I wonder if those are the only human words that I will hear today.

What would happen if I just walked out the door? Somehow, I find myself in the room used for drawing blood from the research participants. There the blood is, rolling away on the rocker. I pick up a biohazard bag and a rubber glove, place the specimen in the bag, and walk back to my deafeningly quiet room. I press the huge switch to flip the power on the enormous centrifuge.

Carefully, I place the sample in a canister and balance the canister opposite it with a similar tube filled with water. The speed is set to 1200 rpm, so I turn the dial to ten minutes. The machine begins to thump and rock like it is going to explode. Fear that I don't know what the hell I am doing overwhelms my every pore. Quickly, I turn the dial back to zero time. Opening the lock, I look inside of each canister to find a big tube of water that I absentmindedly left there.

Once again, I start the timer. Ten minutes seem like ten hours, as I surf the Internet. It is so hard to believe that I have spent five hours in this room all alone with not one thing to do. They told me this when they hired me, but the reality is more grueling than the fantasy.

What is the most grueling is that so much has happened in my life since last year, and I have no one to share it with while I am here. My life seems to begin when the clock at work stops. Then I can talk to my fellow friends that are certified peer specialists. We all met in Helen, Georgia, at training. In telling our stories to each other, I found a sense of peace that was unlike singing in the choir. Together, we shared our struggle and understood each other so well.

I regret that I could only work as a certified peer specialist for a month before my credit card debt started rearing its ugly head. I had to put down all my newfound life experience and take up the research skills I learned in school. Research seems so soulless because I can't express all the rich life experience I've had to my colleagues. They just wouldn't understand and might shove me out of this job in fear.

What was so great is that I had finally realized I was a wife, a daughter, a granddaughter, a friend, an aunt, an artist, a gardener, a cook, a swimmer, and a writer. All these things I knew before, but they weren't as essential in defining my life. Now they were everything. I would try to remember hymns from my church as I worked. "I release and let go, let the spirit run my life...." Over the years, I had spent so much of my life listening to the words of the spiritual counselors at my church on Sundays. One even wrote me a letter to say that she was praying for me. All this would help, but there was nothing like being able to open up to someone that had been in my shoes.

My cell phone rings.

"Hello?"

"Hi, this is the Department of Human Resources: Division of Mental Health, Developmental Disabilities, and Addictive Diseases. I'm Gwen Skinner's secretary; she is the director of the Division. I'm calling to schedule an interview with you for the position as the Director of Consumer Relations and Recovery."

"Wow," I said. "Umm ... that would be great!"

"Can you come to 2 Peachtree on the twenty-eighth of September?"

"Yes, can it be at five p.m.?"

"I'll check on that and call you back, okay? I think that Larry is coming down, and it will be difficult to contact him, but I'll call you back." It was Larry Fricks's job that I had applied for. He was one of the great founders of the Certified Peer Specialist training and a national consumer leader.

"Great!"

I almost forget about the blood. I open the canister and pull out the tube, only to find that the blood serum has turned pink. I draw out the pink serum and place it in the tube. The system spits out the label, and I walk the sample down to the freezer room in the basement. It is like a dungeon, but I am warmed today by the reality that I have been chosen for an interview for Larry Fricks's old job.

I just know Larry, really, I don't know his job so well. He is such an inspiring person. To even be considered to be somewhere near where he was is an honor. The sky seems bluer and the clouds whiter, the window seems even bigger. The cars beyond the trees beckon me to come out and play. Faithfully, I file the sample in the freezer kept at eighty degrees below zero and wait out my moments till I can clock out.

On my way out the door, I called Jayme, my friend and Webmaster for Georgia's Certified Peer Specialist Project. "Jayme, it's Carol. I need your help."

"Is something wrong?"

"No, something is right."

"I need your help getting ready for an interview for the director of Consumer Relations and Recovery Section with the Division."

"Meet me at the Varsity, okay?" she said, referring to a convenient restaurant.

"Thanks, Jayme!"

I hadn't seen Jayme in ages, but if the Webmaster couldn't help me, who would?

The sound of cooking and orders for their landmark necked dogs and French fries were booming in the background as I awaited my friend in front of the ice cream stand. I was slurping the end of a frozen cola when she came around the corner, beaming.

"Jayme, how are you?" I said, as we hugged hello.

"Great! Let's walk up the street to the Spotted Dog. They've got great food for a bar."

"Sounds good."

We made our way to the old firehouse that housed the bar. A blond hostess sat us outside. The wind was blowing Jayme's red hair back and forth as we eyed the menu.

"I think I'm going to have the shepherd's pie. That sounds so good," Jayme said.

"Perhaps I'll get the spinach and goat cheese pizza, and we can split them," I suggested.

"That's a great idea!"

"So what can you tell me about this job?"

"This is more than a job. This is a life in itself. Are you sure you're ready for all this?" Jayme said.

"What do you mean?"

"Everyone will be looking to you for leadership. Can you be a leader?"

"Yes," I said. "I already lead a support group with the Depression and Bipolar Support Alliance. I'm not an authoritarian ruler or anything. I am very democratic about how I run the group. I lead in a gentle way."

"That's so good to hear. Have you heard about everything going on? I think that they could really use someone like you."

"What is going on?" I asked.

"It's just not a good time in mental health. There are all kinds of cutbacks." She frowned as she spoke.

"I'm a frugal person. I think that I can handle that," I said confidently.

"Can you commute to downtown?" she asked.

"Yes, I've done that almost my whole career. I went to Georgia State for my bachelor's degree. I always used to be in the car for forty-five minutes to get somewhere."

"I know you're going to be just perfect for the job. I can feel it." Her blue eyes lit up as she spoke.

"Really?" I asked

"Yes."

Our food came, and we picked at it as Jayme told me her good news.

"Do you know how long I have live in supported housing?" she asked.

"How long?"

"Forever, and I'm moving! I'm going to move into my own apartment in the suburbs. I've got just enough money to do it. I'm so excited. Where I live is so dangerous. I can't wait to get out there and be on my own! It's such a big step."

"You're right! Congratulations! That is so exciting!" I said.

"They have nature trails, an exercise room, a dishwasher, and a Kroger right across the street!"

"I'm so happy for you. I read that chapter of your book you were talking about on the Free-For-All board."

"You did. Did you like it?" Jayme asked.

"Yes, I've never been bound before. Is it true?"

"It's fiction, but I've been shackled in a paddy wagon before."

"What?"

"Yes, I was picked up off the street one time. I was shackled in a paddy wagon with all these other people for two hours before going to the hospital. They wouldn't even let us go to the bathroom."

"That's so inhumane," I said. "I never knew you could be shackled just because you are mentally ill."

"It's true. Just the other day, Virginia stood up at the Carter Center and said that she wanted to know who was going to do something about the shackling of the mentally ill in transport which happens every day in Georgia."

"I can't believe that. That is so horrible. You were at the Carter Center? I'm so envious."

"Well, you'll be talking to Rosalyn Carter from now on. She calls the Georgia Mental Health Consumer Network all the time."

"Really?" I asked. "That is so amazing. I can't believe this! I hope they pick me, and even if they don't, it will be such an honor just to be interviewed."

"You're going to get the job. I can feel it," Jayme assured me.

We parted ways on North Avenue and made our way home.

A fantastic idea came to me in my sleep. There could be an art exhibit that combined recovery principles and art. Artists that had found wellness could paint pictures of hope to draw in the community to the recovery movement.

9

My Mirror

It was like staring into a mirror as he breathlessly muttered the truth that kept him alive and mysteriously marked the end of everything. My life was so at peace now, compared to the time at which I was feeling what he was describing.

"I know someone in the CIA," he gulped as his elbow collapsed on the edge of his large coffee cup. The brown fountain spewed up and then drooled from the table to the floor. "But I can't really tell you about that."

"I believe you." I looked him in the eye and shook my head. "Why don't you sit over here?" I motioned to the dry chair opposite me as he mopped his lap with napkins.

"This is all so crazy, and some people I say this to believe me. Other people just look at me like I've lost it and walk away." He hopped up and moved to the chair with barely a thought of the brown fountain. He continued to speak as if the spill had never happened.

"You're looking at me like you believe there is a kernel of truth to my theory of the universe," he said. "There is so much more to tell you. So much more than you know that I can't tell you."

The brown liquid had now pooled on the floor, but no one around us seemed to notice.

"If I share my knowledge with you, your marriage will be in jeopardy and your husband will want to kill me," he continued. His eyes penetrated mine with a sense of absolute desperation.

"I see. I guess it is not a good idea that you share this with me, but there is something I must tell you. There was a time when I saw connections to everything around me, and it got to be so horrifying that I fled for my life. Some would say that you are a genius, and others would say you are ill. Only you know the truth."

"It is the truth!" He was frustrated by my words.

"It is your truth. I believe you, but it is your personal truth."

"Yes, it is my truth." His eyes lit with understanding.

"Just know that if you get so far away from everyone and everything that you can't trust anybody, you can take medication and come back," I said, searching his eyes for understanding.

"*No!* I really must go. You have understood me and proven my theory. I just don't know how we should contact each other: my cell, e-mail? No. We should leave it like this, because you and your husband share the very secret of the universe that I am talking about, and you don't want to leave him." His trembling hand gestured my understanding.

"No," he continued. "We should leave it this way. I've got to get back to work. I could lose my job, though my boss understands me. I couldn't really lose my job. I could lose everything with this theory, you see. I know if I pursue this, I will die. I'm going to go home and type this up on the Internet. I keep track of everything on the Internet. Look up my name if you want to call me. It's Nick Ishmael," he said, pressing his words rapidly from his lips.

"Don't you think you should keep up with me, so I can help you with your theory? I can see you on 'Secret TV' with the secret of the universe. Have you seen that Web site on the Internet? Your theory would be perfect. I can see you on there with your book!" I was so excited about the possibilities.

I continued, "And all you have said is at the crux of everything that I do in my work and in my life. My work *is* my life. You could come to the support group that I run and meet other people that see connections in the universe. They mostly think that they are living with a diagnosis or problem, unlike you, but you could meet some people with similar experiences." I knew he would not go for this, but I had to try.

"*No!* I think your other suggestion was on par. I should explore this theory. I may lose everything. Don't call me. It's better this way. I can't give you my phone number because your husband may find it, and he would kill me." Anxiety was set in his wide eyes.

"I don't think that my husband is going to kill you. And you should really think about coming to the writer's group because they will listen to your ideas and critique them." I spoke in the most reassuring tone I could muster as I stared at my empty tea cup.

"*No!* Your husband won't like it if I am talking to you. Doesn't that make sense? Men and women cannot be friends." His tone was adamant.

"That all makes sense in an archetypal way, but not in reality." I was dismayed.

"I've had so many strange experiences. You wouldn't believe me if I told you about them."

"Try me."

"Once I was visiting the room of my deceased brother, and I had a vision of us running through a field, but it was real. You see, this is all part of my theory. I've had many experiences like this." His eyes peered into mine as if he was searching for some type of answer.

"There is a name in the medical world for what you're experiencing, but I shouldn't tell you," I said.

"What? Tell me." He spoke with a confident tone that begged me to lay it all out.

"I'm not a doctor. I can't really diagnose you. The name means so little. We are all so much more than the labels that are imposed upon us. It's just that you sound so much like me at one time." I looked away.

"Tell me," he pleaded. "I have to know."

"The medical world would probably say that you're experiencing bipolar disorder, and others would say you're a genius."

"I'm not a genius. And I've heard that before," he said.

As I glanced at my watch, he spurted out, "Okay, I've got to get back to work, and I see you do, too."

"Are you sure you don't want to give me your number or something?" I said as I stood up from my chair.

We had the same circular conversation about my husband killing him all the way to the door, and once we had breached the double doors of the bookstore, I tried to make one last impression on him.

"You know, Nick, I could die just walking down the street. You could die just driving home in your car." I smiled sincerely.

"You're right. Don't let anything happen to you." He turned and walked into the wind away from the door.

"I won't," I replied to his backward glance before he disappeared toward the parking lot in the back of the store.

As I drove my little white Honda home, I looked down the sidewalk he had traveled down. There was no one.

I reflected on all that I was in the middle of in my career, and it spanned in and out of his story about world peace.

Just the day before, I had stood before 350 mental health consumers and their families at the old train depot near the Capitol, pouring out the truth nearest to my soul. "I am Carol Coussons de Reyes, Director of Consumer Relations and

Recovery Section of Mental Health Developmental Disabilities and Addictive Disease from the Department of Human Resources," I said.

"Today I want to welcome you to Mental Health Day at the Capitol with the lyrics from a song with sign language. *Love in any language straight from the heart brings us all together.*" The audience applauded. "When we act in love and not fear, we can accomplish anything. We can conquer parity. We can conquer health disparities … and, in love, I would like to welcome you to Mental Health Day at the Capitol." I exited the stage with the thrill that I hadn't lost my breath or stumbled upon my words or signing. Sherri Jenkins Tucker, head of the Georgia Mental Health Consumer Network, smiled at me with warmth.

I kissed both my parents good-bye, in wonder that they appeared over and over in my work now. I picked up my coat and walked past the tables, smiling and greeting my colleagues and friends. Ironically, I passed one of my best friends from high school. She smiled and hugged me with sincerity. I exited the depot and walked through a cloud of my frozen breath across the streets above Underground Atlanta.

The crowd was thick at the Five Points Marta station. Amid the voices and music from the restaurants, I walked toward 2 Peachtree Street, to my office on the twenty-third floor overlooking the I-75 and I-85 connection.

From here, there is so much to accomplish: training future consumer leaders to carry the torch of hope to other consumer leaders, promoting consumer-run programs, nurturing the partnership between my section and the Georgia Mental Health Consumer Network, meeting with NAMI and the Georgia Bureau of Investigation and the police to bring about Crisis Intervention Training, reaching out to mental health consumers wherever they are, reducing stigma and discrimination, designing new services, and transforming the mental health system to recovery with my fellow Certified Peer Specialists.

The movement to create change in the community doesn't only lie in my hands; my parents have taken it up, too. My parents attended events with the National Alliance on Mental Illness in their small southern community. My father has taken it upon himself to volunteer to help me in my work whenever he can. I ask, and he is there. Today, he is in central Georgia looking for a local coffee shop for an art exhibit by individuals that live with mental health issues.

What keeps me on this side of reality in the year 2007 is my husband, my peers, and my job. If I didn't think I could change this world, I believe my soul would be running to the reality that I can create all for myself. Since I can fight demons and find love in the real world, I don't have to travel to the other side to find them.

My personal secret of good health, aside from a wellness plan, is having an intimate partner that is looking out for my best interests. He knows I have been through a lot. My husband wants me to be safe and secure. His faith has brought me closer to my own spirituality. Our cultural differences sometimes lead us to a place where words fail us, yet we seem to always persevere and rise above when we go to God in prayer.

The church that blessed our marriage has brought us so much life. They offer us not only counsel but also a family of other couples in our community that value marriage. My husband slowly led me back to God's voice through the Catholic Church, and that it was my peers that made me ready to hear him.

My peers help me make sense of all that does not make sense in this world and I do not know what I would do without them. We cry together, laugh together, and discuss things that individuals that have not walked in our shoes can not fully appreciate. My peers know what it is like to be considered a second-class citizen and to have your basic human rights taken from you. Together we focus on our strengths, search for answers to empower the next generation, and remember those that have walked before us.

It is important to feel that I can change the planet we live on. My work allows me to influence change in the world of mental health issues. It is a dream job, and it seems like magic that the pieces of my life came together so that I could live in this spot on the planet today.

Peace and Love,
Carol

10

Peace

There is peace in my heart today: peace that is like never before. It is miraculous. Here I will lay down the words of my peace that belongs to me, while I can share them with you—no one, not anyone, can take that peace from me. Only I can give it away.

There is a word in my world that is often misunderstood and hated by some: spirituality. It is remarkable that I can feel this sensation inside and outside of my body. This sensation or experience is what my friend, Lorishka, tried to give to me when I was young when she urged me to "meditate" during times of great problems. Often I would try to meditate as she commanded and feel nothing.

Years later, my father signed both of us up for a yoga class. I found that I was so relaxed that I could actually look at other people in their eyes and not have fear. Looking at people, eye to eye, was extremely difficult for me as a teen. For years this relaxation I felt in yoga had a powerful influence on my ability to focus my thoughts and even approach the notion of meditation.

If you have read the previous chapters with a human heart, you may have seen the evolution of my spirituality forming in my great struggle. I did not lie down and die when faced with the rejection of the world, I reached out to touch life again: to meet the world eye to eye.

This touch with the humanity of my own story inside and the story of my peers has left me with profound feelings and questions. How do I live with all of this knowledge, all of these stories, and all of this wisdom? Connection with all of this hurts in some ways as much as it heals, because my connections with people in my lifetime have been painful and have hurt.

I went to church with a connected but bleeding and wounded heart. In this church, I found a priest that weekly asked us what we do to embrace the poor. I began to see that while my heart is bleeding, I am still standing and I live very well compared to my peer that I pass on the street on the way to my climate-controlled office. In his words about the suffering of the poor from the pain of things like rejection, great hunger, and physical discomfort—I realized that these individuals are living moments of great meaning. Their lives are speaking volumes about the whole of humanity, just as each of our lives do.

We all suffer, though some of us suffer from a lack of connection to our fellow man without even realizing it. There are people that do not realize that there are people eating out of garbage cans and sleeping on concrete streets in America. While I can not heal the suffering of the world, I can look and see it squarely in the eyes.

I can greet my fellow man with care and buy him lunch with a smile, when he comes to me on the street. The smile he returns is one that is blackish with the stubs of remaining teeth and I can see the many years that it took for his teeth to wear away. He freely grins showing his teeth to me, offering a vision of his pain to be honored and also a vision of joy to celebrate in connecting. So, I tell him a story of hope about a man I know that once walked the streets like him and he smiles as we connect. Suddenly, my time is gone in these situations and my life with my work or my husband calls me to walk away. I carry what he has taught me with me.

While many people blame the plight of the homeless on the closing of mental institutions, I cannot imagine asking any of them to live in the institutions that I have passed through. I don't think that building communities of separation are ever the answer. We need to connect to each other, we need to connect to all types of people: angry, sad, ecstatic, happy, imaginative, talkative, or silent. The only way to connect to others is to be in touch with our own heart's journey.

I cannot feed everyone on the streets. I cannot listen to everyone on the streets. I can look them in the eye and listen for a moment. I can listen to the stories of my husband, of my peers, my friends, and those I serve to connect to them. I can tell my story to anyone that will listen. I can give part of my income to people that serve people on the streets. I can honor my peers that have suffered from our human inability to connect to those that are different. I can dream. I can pray. This is what I can do.

It is these connections and not everything that distracts us from them that are at the heart of life. My dreams may require money, but the only ones that are essential are those that bring me closer to people. While wearing a beautiful suit may help me to gain connection to some people, what do I really gain that is meaningful? Perhaps I gain income from that suit, but the suit itself will not comfort me when I am afraid. The words of those I connect to will.

So, in the great and wonderful mystery of the world I have fallen off the beaten path a bit in my journey today. I have lived a Christmas without a Christmas tree. This would bring sadness to many, but to me it brought peace. I realized that this tree was shining brightly in my husband's eyes and the love that we receive from those around us. I realized that love is not in any store, but in the soft straw of a manger. Love is in this hope.

In the spirit of practicing good science, my doctor has taken me off my medications so that I may have a body that would not be toxic to the birth of a child. In faith and trust, my spiritual guide at church has lifted my spirit to see how miraculous it is that I have been well for many months. While I am not a prophet, I know that this time is different than any other time in my life. I know that I will never be perfect. I do not have all the answers, but I know I am living the most sacred prayer I could speak. This is a journey that no mortal man or woman can lead, we can only listen.

About the Author

My expertise in the mental health arena comes from a variety of places. I have a bachelor's degree in psychology from Georgia State University and a master's degree in psychology from Augusta State University. Over the years, I have participated in research, taught at a university, worked as a counselor, and collaborated with a team of professionals as a staff psychologist. I have written and published papers and made presentations at conferences. More recently and most valuable, I have been trained as a Certified Peer Specialist in Georgia. Currently, I work as the director of Consumer Relations and Recovery for the State of Georgia with DHR:DMHDDAD. I am also a member of the National Association of Consumer Survivor Mental Health Administrators and our statewide coordinator for the Campaign for Mental Health Recovery. Over the years, I have learned many truths, and this is what I have to share with you.

As an undergraduate, I was passionate to learn more about mental health. I grew up with a friend who was labeled with schizophrenia by doctors. His art intrigued me and left me constantly guessing about how to interpret his mind. At the same time, I was suffering through great darkness myself. I remember how I connected with this friend about my desire to commit suicide. Though I had many questions to answer about my own life, I went to college with a desire to cure schizophrenia. When I expressed this desire to my professors about my friend, they reinforced my caring for this friend. I studied chemistry but found myself lost. I knew I would have a hard time designing a drug to cure my friend. My grades were better in psychology, and my therapist recommended that I stick with what I was good at. I embarked on a path to attempt to attain a Ph.D. in psychology.

One day, I made a presentation in a neuropsychology course on schizophrenia and presented an original piece of art given to me by my friend. I talked about the frontal lobe of the brain and its role in schizophrenia. After an extensive discussion of the biology of the brain and how it related to behavior, I presented my friend's art as a demonstration of how one could visualize the illness. There were worms coming in and out of the body and religious symbols. My instructor said, "What if this was just the work of an artist?" He went on to describe the talent of a man he knew who made angels that were quite popular. The man had been labeled with a mental illness. The instructor warned me about the damage labeling people can have.

From that day forward, I was horrified when I saw people labeled. I volunteered at a psychiatric psychosocial rehabilitation center where there were many gentlemen who lived with schizophrenia. What I remember most from this experience was that many of the people who were served by this community would introduce themselves in a weekly meeting saying, "I am so and so, I am schizophrenic, and my medications are Haldol, Cogentin, and ..." I was so disturbed that the treatment team would sit around and listen to this week after week. I knew it seemed wrong that they would label themselves week after week, but I didn't know quite what to do.

Another thing that bothered me was the side effects of the medications. Those who took the older drugs seemed to have motor tics such as repetitive arm movements or muscular jerks. I also saw people balloon up quickly on some of the newer drugs. Though I didn't realize the possible connection between the new drugs, weight gain, and diabetes at the time, I was struck by the number of people with diagnoses of insulin or non-insulin-dependent diabetes. Secretly I wondered what was worse, people with unusual behaviors or these side effects. The doctors, my training, and my desire to help individuals were louder than the tape playing in the background of my mind about the side effects of these drugs.

I will say to those who do not have awareness of an experience of being around individuals with mental health issues that the worst thing that happened to me in my three years as a volunteer at the center was that someone touched my foot. It may seem simple to you, but it was a big deal to me. I was doing a survey on smoking and antipsychotic medications in individuals with schizophrenia. I sat next to a gentleman at a picnic table.

He said, "Will you take off your shoe?"

I said, "No, we are outside, and I need it."

He said, "I want to see what brand it is."

In my own materialistic world, this made perfect sense, so I said, "Okay." I removed my shoe to look inside, and immediately his hand traced the bottom of my foot. Quickly, I replaced my shoe, finished the survey, and ran inside. I felt a deep division between wanting to like this person and trying to understand something that had offended me.

Too often in our society, we get offended by people with unusual behavior before we learn what they have to offer us. One common theme I saw among most of these individuals is that everyone talked about wanting a job. This always inspired me. I wanted to know how people could not just be satisfied with their disability checks when they suffered so. I wondered what drove them to want to get into the workforce and earn money, so I did some research.

I remember reading that our society values individuals for the money that they earn. Also, this article said individuals with serious mental illnesses have lower incomes and that many live in poverty. I became angry that our society would value people based on the dollars that they can make.

As a student, I remember being embarrassed about my own experiences with sadness. One day, I excused myself to cry in the bathroom because I was so moved by a story that had the rest of the class laughing in English literature. Another day, I broke down in tears in front of my French teacher because students were cheating on their oral exams. I cried myself to sleep at night often and slept through many of my classes.

My experiences were made worse by drinking and my concerns over an experience that is referred to as "cutting." I was in so much pain as I reflected on my life that I would take a knife and make small cuts on my arm. The pain would make me feel better, it was reassurance that I was still alive. I sought out a counselor from the university, because I was afraid.

This counselor felt my issues would better be served by the psychology clinic but said due to my major it would be a bad idea for my to receive care there. After three sessions and having me sign a contract that I would go to an emergency room if I thought about hurting myself, he ended our sessions. His recommendation was that I see a therapist with my father's insurance on me. I talked to my father and he refused to let me call the insurance company. I told this to the counselor from my school and he said there was nothing that he could do.

After a year, I became suicidal and I rebelled against his decision and called the insurance company. I saw a therapist and hid my experiences from everyone else around me. I couldn't bring myself to study depression because it made me feel hopeless.

After two years of therapy, my doctors wanted me to take an antidepressant, but I was afraid of medications because I knew that all we knew about the brain was mostly theory. I knew that all those movies about how the brain worked were not 100 percent real. Another reservation I had was that my doctors said that I would have to take this medication for the rest of my life. I was quick to tell them that I learned in psychopharmacology courses that medications were only tested by the government for a few months and that there was no testing to say what the long-term effects of the drugs were.

It took weeks to compromise with my doctors. They influenced me with research that said the medication must be taken for at least nine months to have lasting effects. When I first started taking it, I thought I would die. I had dizziness that made me an unsafe driver, and I could barely walk from table to table in my job as a restaurant hostess. I remember thinking that my life was better before, when I could drive and work with a clear mind. Also, I began to wonder what life was worth.

One day during the first few weeks of the medication, I was sitting with my mother, and I collapsed against the couch. Tears began to roll down my cheek because I wanted to move and I could not. This lasted for several minutes. Afterward, I told my mother what I was experiencing, and we immediately went to my health care provider.

They asked me questions such as what day it was and if I had been hospitalized before. They then proceeded to hand over the Physician's Desk Reference. They opened it up and said, "Look, these are the side effects. What you are saying is not listed there."

From there, I was sent home with a big question mark lingering over my head. I did quit taking it, but out of desperation and hope I started taking it, again, on my birthday. After taking an antidepressant for nine months, I became happy and interested in life. That was not the only influence I had on my health, I also decided to pursue a dream of becoming a clinical psychology professor. I moved to a new city and worked on my master's degree.

At Augusta State University, I found everything I wanted to know about psychology and more. I learned that the origin of labeling mental illnesses dated back to a time when people were being accused of witchcraft. Doctors came along and said that people that were considered possessed had epilepsy. Slowly doctors came to label more and more unpopular behaviors. At one point in the history of the Diagnostic and Statistical Manual, homosexuality was even considered a diagnosis.

Reading articles about Freud, I learned that he had really let women down in our society. He had an opportunity to speak out publicly about the fact that the women he was treating with psychoanalysis were sexually abused. Before he could say this, his peers spoke against such a notion, and he changed his theory to say that these women were fantasizing. I will never consider Freud a genius because of that.

Finally, I learned about the work of Dr. Thomas Szasz and how he felt that mental illness was a myth. This radical psychiatrist can be found today, still speaking to the dangers of labeling people in our society. Although I loved reading his work and found some of what he said undeniable, I was unsure what to think of this man. He seemed a little radical.

My research skills flourished in my work with the local Department of Veteran's Affairs medical center and the Medical College of Georgia. I studied migraine headaches and relaxation therapy, coded behaviors and emotions, learned about panic attacks and breathing retraining, and then I stumbled upon essential fatty acids.

My landlord said he knew a researcher who needed someone to participate in his work in exchange for getting data for their thesis project. I was unsure of what to do for my graduate school thesis, so I called this biochemist. He invited me into the world of essential fatty acids research. He was concerned about the side effects of medications that people take for schizophrenia and attention deficit hyperactivity disorder. As a result of his concern, he was interested in the influence that essential fatty acids have on behavior.

He mostly studied with mice but wanted to expand his research to children. Essential fatty acids (EFAs) had been found in brain tissue and also certain foods, like green leafy vegetables and salmon. In our modern world of fast food, people often do not eat enough fish and vegetables. With a study of a thousand children with attention deficit hyperactivity disorder, this researcher remarked that we could easily make the cover of the *New England Journal of Medicine*. I began to unravel the details of how to complete this study.

As an undergraduate, I read the book *Emotional Intelligence* and was convinced that true changes in our society must come from working with children. Until I met up with the biochemist, I had no idea how to focus my work on children. The pieces came together, and I found myself with a week-long diet diary, appointments with the principals of several elementary schools, a budget for food, a one-page assessment for ADHD symptoms for parents and teachers, and a computer program to analyze diets.

With modest results, I found myself somewhat shy of the evidence required for a prestigious peer-review journal. After I finished my graduate school thesis, I found myself looking for a job. The only one available was working with the Department of Vocational Rehabilitation in South Carolina. With a mental health caseload, I began work as a counselor with the goal of employing individuals with disabilities in the community. This work was very rewarding. Finally, I was able to help people with disabilities get what many of them wanted so badly—a place in the American workforce. I was promoted to staff psychologist and found myself writing psychological reports to assist people with disabilities.

In this position, I was to label people with mental health issues, addictive diseases, or developmental disabilities so that they would be eligible for services. I worked hard to do this the right way, though it was difficult in the face of a constant demand to work faster. I had to stand my ground and refuse to make guesses about behaviors that had standardized tests to measure them. I really felt like I was helping people turn their lives around and get help from their local mental health centers.

I found myself advocating for individuals' needs. Sometimes the local mental health center would refuse to refill a prescription because someone had taken their medication incorrectly or lost it. Some individuals were released from the hospital without enough medication to get them to their next appointment. I would make phone calls and rationalize with their treatment teams. I usually got results.

At the same time, I began teaching at the local university. Teaching Psychology 101 was so much fun. I loved to talk about theories, neurochemicals, and behavior. The students were often wild, and I would get in trouble for having rowdy classes. At the same time, the students seemed to really appreciate what I had to say. Then, something happened one day that changed all our lives.

I walked into the university and saw students staring at a TV screen. I simply assumed the war scene was Afghanistan and ran up the stairs to get my mail. The office secretary exclaimed, "Have you heard what is happening?"

"No," I said.

"You need to go home and turn on your television right away."

"Why?" I asked. I didn't watch television because it made me sad and wasted my time.

"There are terrorists in New York City! You need to go home and learn about germ warfare and get prepared!" she exclaimed.

I don't remember much more about the conversation, but I went home and did not turn on the television. I had lessons to write, papers to grade, the Graduate Record Exam to study for, my job to do at vocational rehabilitation, and my best friend to visit in the hospital, where she was recovering from a heart attack. On top of all that, I was taking a stimulant for attention deficit hyperactivity disorder—inattentive type. The event didn't exist in my mind. I didn't have time to grieve with the nation. All the flags I saw were like something from a movie, detached and odd. The worst part was that I let down my students by not bringing up one discussion on the topic.

One night, I was returning from the university, and I found myself driving on the median. I thought I was on the road, and I still don't understand how I got there. This was when I realized that I was pushing myself too hard and that something needed to give soon.

Time passed, and I found myself in an uncomfortable situation at the vocational rehabilitation where a co-worker seemed to be sexually harassing me. Then a miracle happened: the Department of Veterans Affairs Medical Center invited me to interview for a job studying essential fatty acids and bipolar disorder, as well as schizophrenia. I jumped at the opportunity.

There, I found myself analyzing data, interviewing people with diagnostic assessments, and writing papers. It was hard work for me, as the veterans I worked with suffered greatly from situations I had never seen before. I wasn't a counselor; my role was to study them—to be detached and impartial but friendly. I felt empty because I was not able to assist them but instead just recorded their behavior, entered the numbers, and saw them again in a few weeks. I had so much more to say to each of them. I wrote a paper entitled: *RA Hints and Tips Column: Hotel California (a commentary on bipolar disorder).*

That is where this story began for me. I found myself writing a book to fill up the emptiness in my life. I speak of that work often in this story. It contains great pain, love, and things deep inside me that no one wanted to hear. I found myself writing to the spirit of a friend that I had left behind after my therapist encouraged me to let her go.

This is where this current work you have read starts. It includes diary entries made at that time. Next, the book took you directly into the time in my life when I was walking into what I refer to as another reality and what doctors refer to as psychosis. Doctors always told me that when an individual has mood swings, the up-swing can go so far that an individual becomes fearful and sees the world in a way that others cannot. For some, this different vision of the world is a powerful experience which can be likened to spirituality—like the vision of a shaman. For others, it is a sign of a great illness that is to be eradicated from humanity.

My professional life did not end when my personal experience with mental health issues began. I did avoid my career for awhile, figuring I had nothing left to give anyone. I moved to Atlanta and, after a year, I landed a job at a local university studying domestic violence. My doctors felt safe in taking me off some of my medications, and I decided on my own to go off all my medicines. Then I encountered some unusually difficult stress at work and fell into another world. I began to write again, which is Chapter Two. I recently added some descriptions, because the editors complained I wasn't giving the reader enough details.

Time passed, and I began to learn about support groups. I started a Depression and Bipolar Support Alliance chapter, because there wasn't one close to my house. The fundamentals of the group taught me to focus on my strengths. I also learned that my peers had a lot to teach me about living. Together, we shared how we managed to work, date, participate in hobbies, and talk to our doctors. We talked about our experiences with medications and life in general.

Before I began this group, I learned about the role of a Certified Peer Specialist in the mental health community. When I engaged in training, I was relieved that I had finally found a place that I could envision working. The training emphasized that we are not our labels, that we are not our medication, that we are not our treatment. We talked about how debilitating the medical model can be to an individual's spirit. Moreover we explored firsthand how a recovery model can change people's lives by giving them hope of leading a life in the community again.

The recovery model frightens some people because they think it implies a complete reversal of all behavior that could be considered symptoms by a doctor. This is so scary for people because they think it is impossible for this to occur, that it brings false hope to people, and that it ensures that the individual will again live with mental illness.

What they don't realize is that the word "recovery" means something different to each individual. For some, it means living with medication for the rest of their lives. For others, it means engaging in psychotherapy without medication. It can also mean finding the confidence to be one's self with meditation, exercise, and peer-support. Let your mind wander as to what this can mean for the individual, for it is infinite in specific meanings.

What the recovery model allows for is individual voice, and this is quite frightening for many. Many do not want individuals to be able to choose their medication; they think that only a doctor can do this. The truth is that doctors today need input from those they serve to do their jobs effectively.

The recovery model also emphasizes that people can make choices about where they want to live. People don't typically like to live in hospitals. Most people share the American dream of owning their own homes, as well as their own lives. Many individuals with mental health issues, like myself (smile), are living this dream today.

Another great thing about recovery is that individuals can be people and not illnesses. When we take off our labels, we find we are artists, poets, mothers, brothers, uncles, aunts, teachers, authors, doctors, etc. The possibilities are endless. When we focus on these positive roles and not the role of being ill, we find strength and connection with humanity.

The recovery model allows one to engage civil rights that date back to the Declaration of Independence and with our humanity that began at the beginning of man. I've been told I could have sued my parents and doctors for hospitalizing me against my will when I was not a danger to myself or others. Today, many individuals with mental health issues are realizing that they have civil rights. They are engaging lawyers and the courts to protect those rights. Those that have been successful have left an imprint in the development and planning of treatment in many states.

Another truth is that, without input from those they serve, doctors can do great damage. Look at the history of the lobotomy. In research, only significant findings (or in other words, things that work) often get published in journals. So, only the doctors that had performed lobotomies with successful results were published. The truth that the results of these surgeries were quite horrifying was not found in scientific journals. It was discovered when doctors would talk to each other at scientific meetings about how things weren't working out so well for them.

Today, we have people with mental health issues meeting in support groups, in peer support programs, and at conferences talking about the treatment they receive. We discuss our history, our connection, our wellness, what is working and not working with each other. We are presenting papers, writing books, and researching how to empower people to make their own decisions about what works best for them in their own personal recovery.

After my training in the recovery model from the Georgia Certified Peer Specialist Project, I wanted to work as a peer specialist. I found myself returning to work as a researcher for financial reasons. I chose biological areas to focus on and left behind everything I had learned in my training in mental health. I studied diabetes, cholesterol, high blood pressure, and HIV. I told no one at work about my lived experience with mental health issues. Finally, I landed upon an unusual opportunity.

The Department of Human Resources: Division of Mental Health, Developmental Disabilities, and Addictive Diseases hired me as the director of Consumer Relations and Recovery. In this position, I am valued not only for my master's degree in psychology, but more importantly for my lived experience with mental health issues. At the division, I represent the consumer voice in meetings and planning at the state level. I also supervise the directors of two programs: the Georgia Certified Peer Specialist Project and the Georgia Peer Support Institute.

In my first year in this position, I feel I have accomplished more than in my entire previous career. Often the territory I walk in is uncharted, but I am able to move boldly forward because I am surrounded by peers living with mental health issues. You may already know the names of some of these individuals, and others are relatively unknown. I think that my doctors could begin to truly understand me, if they knew more about Larry Fricks, Joseph Rogers, Dr. Dan Fisher, Jacki McKinney, Gail Bluebird, Dr. Jean Campbell, Shery Mead, Peter Ashendon, Mary Ellen Copeland, or Dr. Patricia Deegan.

The next time you pass a hospital with a mental health ward, realize that there are great people inside, and they are coming into the community with great gifts. Inside and outside those walls, the great struggle that people endure also bears the fruit of great leaders in every arena of life.

978-0-595-46596-5
0-595-46596-X

www.ingramcontent.com/pod-product-compliance
Lightning Source LLC
Chambersburg PA
CBHW051437280526
45785CB00003B/1326